C000214613

'A valuable contribution to the esoteric history of Britain.'

Geoff Ward, Mysterious Planet

'Even the sceptical must acknowledge the thorough research and considerable scholarship that have gone into the book.'

Dorset Life

'[Gary] presents a wealth of historical and practical information, while not being shy of delving into the deeper mysteries of this important and curiously neglected archipelago.'

Nicholas Mann, British Mystery School of Avalon

'Gary is one of the most respected researchers and speakers in Wessex and this, his first book, aptly reflects the depth and thoroughness of his research over many years ... This book will become the classic on Portland, so I urge you to walk the sacred Isle of Portland and absorb Gary Biltcliffe's wisdom and insights.'

Peter Knight, Dorset Earth Mysteries Group

'For anyone interested in regional folklore and hidden history this book is very welcome. The author has thoroughly investigated the hidden side of Dorset's Isle of Portland. Using long out of print and unpublished works by Clara King Warry, who wrote much about the folklore, mythology and archaeology of Portland during the first half of the 20th century, Gary has managed to piece together a forgotten history of the Isle.'

Alex Langstone, The Heritage Journal

# The
# Spirit of Portland
## Revelations of a Sacred Isle

*Gary Biltcliffe*

*When a land neglects her legends*
*Sees but falsehood in the past*
*And its people view their sires*
*In the light of fools and liars,*
*Tis a sign of its decline,*
*And its splendours cannot last,*
*Branches that but blight their roots*
*Yield no sap for lasting fruits*

*(Robin George Collinwood)*

Roving
Press

Published by Roving Press Ltd
4 Southover Cottages, Frampton, Dorset, DT2 9NQ, UK
Tel: +44 (0)1300 321531
www.rovingpress.co.uk

All dates in the text are approximate, as historical sources differ.

*The quote on the title page is from philosopher and historian Robin George Collinwood, 1887–1943, source unknown.*

First published 2009 by Roving Press Ltd
Reprinted with corrections 2012

ISBN: 978-1-906651-02-2

British Library Cataloguing in Publication Data
A catalogue record for this book is available from the British Library

All photographs, line drawings and maps are by Gary Biltcliffe unless otherwise stated
Cover design by Gary Biltcliffe

Set in 11.5/13 pt by Beamreach (www.beamreachuk.co.uk)
Printed and bound by Beamreach (www.beamreachuk.co.uk)

# Contents

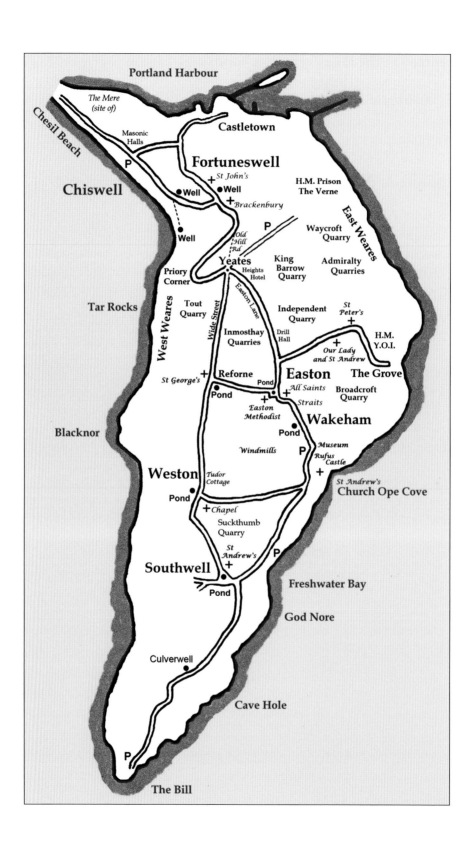

# Acknowledgements

I am grateful to the following people for their help in the making of this book: the late Ian Phelps for opening doors to my quest; Agatha for her support and enthusiasm; Anna-nana for her inspiration and guidance; Jennifer Grierson for her invaluable help with the text; and Mary Kingston and her late husband David for their insights and enthusiasm for the mysteries of Portland.

Thanks also to Brian Clark from the Churches Conservation Trust for permitting me to represent an accurate ground plan of St George's Church by Lewis Brown Chartered Land Surveyors 2007. The opinions and analysis offered by my interpretation of the sacred geometry of St George's Church are mine alone.

Also thanks to all the staff at Portland Museum and Dorset County Museum over the years, Easton Methodist Church and All Saints' Church; all those who gave permission to reproduce some of the photographs in the text; Hannah Sofaer, Paul Crabtree and Mark Pearce from the Drill Hall, whose vision and support have been vital to the book; Stephen for his advice on the Masonic order; and finally my partner Caroline Hoare for her love, help and support in every department of this book.

**Gary Biltcliffe**

# About the Author

Born in 1960, Gary Biltcliffe has dedicated the past 30 years to historical research and investigation of earth mysteries, ancient civilisations and lost knowledge. He has appeared on radio and television and has lectured widely in the UK and North America. He has led international groups around Britain's sacred sites and written articles for local magazines and the Research into Lost Knowledge Organisation. He currently lives in Dorset with his partner Caroline and three cats.

# Reflections

Nearly 2000 copies of *The Spirit of Portland* have sold and the book is now in reprint. Since first publication, many individuals have commented positively on the book, and I would like to thank those who have given feedback and further insights into the many mysteries of the island. The local customs and traditions, unfortunately ignored by today's historians, are an important part of Portland's history, and I hope that by bringing them to people's attention, more people will be inspired by the island, as I have been. I have referred to many secrets hidden in the Portland landscape, one of which is the strange alignment of four churches featured in Chapter 6 and the circles of churches in Chapter 4. Although there are some who have dismissed these alignments and connections out of hand, the facts speak for themselves – they exist whether they like it or not. If indeed they are just a chance arrangement – at odds of thousands to one – then we have something quite miraculous occurring here on Portland.

# Introduction

Some of the earliest esoteric traditions of northern Europe refer to Britain as a place steeped in the supernatural. The ancient Greeks and Romans looked upon our island, surrounded by dangerous dark seas in the western confines of Europe, as the realm and refuge of spirits and magicians.

Free from unwanted physical and psychic influences, the islands that satellite Britain were particularly sacred, as they allowed people to adopt their individual modes of living and practise their own religions and festivals. The great quantity of Neolithic and Bronze Age burial mounds and stone monuments found on these islands is an indication that Britain's earliest inhabitants regarded them as holy. The later Celts referred to them as spiritual abodes of the dead, the resting places of warriors and kings, dedicated to hallowed usage.

Before the advent of Christianity in Britain, the administrators of religion were the Druids, often referred to as the 'teachers of wisdom'. They also gave special reverence to the islands that surrounded their spiritual home, and according to the most ancient history of the British recorded in *The Welsh Triads*[1], Iona, Anglesey, the Isle of Man and the Isle of Wight were major sanctuaries of this priesthood. Many of these islands were under the protection of a specific deity, worshipped by the Druids in woodland groves, at stone pillars and holy wells.

Legend has it that during the first century AD, the teachings of Christ found their way to the British Isles carried by Judean refugees from the Holy Land. The British Druids had foreseen a coming saviour called Hesus and therefore embraced the new teachings, becoming Culdees (from the Irish 'Ceile-De' meaning 'companion' or 'spouse' of God). Many of Britain's islands became safe sanctuaries for the Culdees. Their new monastic communities consisting of clusters of circular huts and an outer wall replaced the shrines and woodland groves of the former Druids.

My research into Portland history, its place names and traditions, reveals that long ago there was a high concentration of stone circles, standing stones, barrows and places associated with the Druids and possibly early Christians. Considering the size of Portland, only 4.5 miles long by 1.75 miles wide, the abnormally large number of ancient monuments speaks volumes for its former sanctity.

I

Portland juts out into the English Channel like a giant wedge, with limestone cliffs standing 500 ft high at its northern end, gradually sloping down to the southerly point called the Bill. Long ago, this impregnable headland had only two places for landing: one at a lagoon called the Mere at the northern extremity of the Isle, now a commercial port; the other at an inlet halfway down the eastern coast called Church Ope Cove. It is certain that the geography of Portland would have appealed to the prehistoric inhabitants living in this area of the country as a strategically safe sanctuary for religious practices or trade.

Portland is technically a peninsular, for it connects to the mainland by an extraordinary bank of pebbles about 18 miles long called Chesil Beach. Yet, many, including myself, still refer to it as an island because, before the building of a road bridge in the nineteenth century, the only visitor access to the peninsular was by ferry, and even this proved to be difficult and often dangerous due to the strong currents of the tidal lake known as the Fleet.

A unique aspect of Portland history is its long and intimate association with royalty. For over a thousand years it has been a Royal Manor with special privileges and rights bestowed on the islanders. This allowed a greater freedom for the Portlanders, without interference from the English Parliament, to practise their individual customs and ways of living, answering only to the King and their governing body, the Court Leet. The latter has continued unimpaired for at least a thousand years to the present day, but its origins could possibly date back another 500 years to the Saxon period when a revolutionary agricultural field system spread over much of the country in the form of the 'open field' system. This was introduced because so much of the arable land in Britain had been abandoned after the plagues during the Dark Ages. The Saxons devised a way for commoners to farm strips of land equally divided within large open fields. They used a 'three-field system' of crop rotation – wheat, barley, fallow. Many of these open fields would be grouped around a village, often with a central green.

Living in relative isolation, with their own laws, the early Portlanders remained separate from the cultural influences, politics and religions of mainland Britain and only married within the island families.

The Victorian period brought a decline to this unique race of people. A constant demand for Portland stone permitted the building of a bridge to replace the ferry as well as new roads and a railway which opened up the interior of the island to intensive quarrying. In addition, a new naval base and prison forced the requisition of a great deal of land, which at the time was rich with prehistoric remains. The resulting population increase in outsiders, called 'Kimberlins' by locals, diluted the old Portland bloodlines and many of their ancient customs and practices died out.

Right up until the early twentieth century, the old island families would teach their children the ancient history of Portland as handed down by their parents and their grandparents before them. Today, mainland historians, who take more heed of the written word than the spoken, ignore these oral traditions, regarding them as mere folklore and myth.

Portland is certainly a place of visual contrast and the densely developed and over-quarried land can make unsightly viewing for the first-time visitor. Yet many locals and visitors have told me that walking the ancient paths around the island gives them a sense of its hidden beauty and sacredness.

Amongst the wealth of literature published on the Isle of Portland, I found that very few touch upon its sacred nature until I came across a number of out-of-print and unpublished works written by a few old Portlanders. One such remarkable author was Mrs Clara King Warry, formerly Clara Jane White (1856–1940), a well-known authority on island folklore and customs. She inherited a legacy of Portland traditions from her grandmother Elizabeth White, formerly Pearce. Her books were a revelation to me, particularly those that relate to the old oral traditions attached to sacred places around the island. It was also clear, after reading these books, that many of the old Portlanders revered their island with a deep understanding of its mystery and heritage that reflects a sense of spirituality and enlightenment. These unique traditions, combined with my experience of travelling and studying early cultures around the world, gave me new insights into the missing areas of British history and our Celtic legacy, particularly the obscure Dark Ages.

After many years exploring the island and studying its folklore, the rocky peninsular began to reveal to me some of its hidden mysteries through a method called geomythics. The term geomythics, first used by the late Anthony Roberts, refers to symbolic truths expressed through stories concerning natural features in the surrounding rural area or landscape. For instance, the elevated area upon which Rufus Castle stands, and the nearby atmospheric ruin of St Andrew's Church above Church Ope Cove seem to hide such a symbolic or factual truth that this area of coastline was once the centre of the island.

Here I received a revelation that led me to discover that from this sacred centre many of the churches and monuments around the island relate to a divine plan that underlies the structure of nature and all living creatures, a plan termed sacred geometry. Historians regard this system of placing buildings as an ancient practice used by the medieval Knights Templars, although my research reveals that on Portland it continued right up to the early part of the twentieth century.

In an attempt to uncover the amazing legacy of sacred Portland, I had to break new ground by combining the study of Portland's archaeology, oral traditions, folklore and the old families with a more open-minded approach to research.

A good deal of my findings took place on foot, so I have included five walking tours at the back of this book to allow the reader to explore many of the sites featured.

*Portland sunset*

# Chapter 1

# Sacred Stone

A sacred landscape is an area of enchantment, a place of power that often draws people without explanation. It is a land often shaped by our ancestors, who recognised something beyond the physical order of nature in the shape of a hill, a rock, or the miraculous flow of a spring of life-giving water. Sacred landscapes have a wealth of folklore, with tales of strange beings such as giants and fairies and events of a paranormal nature. I believe Portland has all the ingredients of a sacred landscape and more, as this book will reveal.

My exploration of Portland begins with the study of the underlying structure, the unique geology or bones of the island, which I believe is a key to unlocking some of the mysteries of the sacred landscape. Portland is most famous for its stone, attracting architects and stonemasons from the time of the Romans in search of good-quality building materials. Portland stone is a sedimentary rock known as oolitic limestone. Oolites are small rounded particles or grains, so named because they look like fish eggs, commonly formed by layers of material, usually calcite, deposited around tiny particles such as quartz, sand or fossil fragments through the rolling motion of the tide in shallow waters.[1]

Millions of years ago, the formation of the island began when a section of seabed rose out of the sea during geological upheaval. The limestone beds vary in different parts of the island and contain many layers rich in fossils, such as the Roach layer. The most sought-after layers are Whitbed and Basebed, ideal building stone. Their even texture and lack of shells make them a joy to carve, with a distinctive white colouring when cut and polished. Beneath the limestone layers are very large deposits of much softer sand and clay, over 200 ft deep in places. This slippery foundation has been the cause of many recorded landslides.

Early cultures from around the world regarded limestone as sacred and symbolic of the physical planes of existence, because it contains layer upon layer of organic sediments formed gradually over millions of years. They viewed sandstone and granite as symbolic of spirit due to their crystalline structure created through cataclysms and tectonic movements. These turbulent changes may have been the result of prehistoric encounters with celestial objects such as comets or meteorites.

Because limestone is softer than igneous rock and easy to extract, the general opinion is that our ancient ancestors gave preference to this stone over others to build their magnificent temples and pyramids throughout the world. However, Dr Philip Callahan states that they may have utilised the stone for its inherent magnetic qualities.[2] Callahan found that all substances are either diamagnetic, meaning repelled by a magnetic field, or paramagnetic, meaning attracted to a magnetic field. Organic material such as plants and water are diamagnetic whereas stone and metals are paramagnetic. Organic soil, with a high concentration of iron-rich clay, is highly fertile as it contains the right balance of diamagnetic and paramagnetic ingredients, like the Chinese yin and yang.

Callahan believes that the megalithic builders and the later Celts who built many of their religious structures from oolitic limestone utilised its qualities to bring balance and harmony to the surrounding landscape. He explains that during its formation, paramagnetic impurities from the precipitation of clay minerals such as manganese and iron emit a weak magnetic field that benefits nature and wildlife. He also adds that:

> *"… under the proper conditions, it [oolitic limestone] will not only conduct electricity, but also amplify cosmic paramagnetic forces."*[2]

Although Callahan's ideas are a blend of interesting academic and alternative theories, it is clear that limestone has unique qualities that go beyond simple ease of carving. Paul Devereux says that the Neolithic builders of the great sarsen (sandstone) and earth temples at Avebury in Wiltshire deliberately used oolitic limestone in their barrows.[3] The dry-stone walling found in West Kennet Long Barrow is a particular example of this. Because oolitic limestone is not native to that area, its use at this site must have had a sacred significance.[3]

Callahan further discovered that Ireland is composed of two types of limestone. One variety, found in the mountainous rim of the country, is harder, more resistant to weathering and highly paramagnetic, whilst the other, found in the subsoil bedrock that underlies the great plain of central Ireland, is diamagnetic. Callahan further discovered that the Irish Celts built their dwellings with insulating diamagnetic limestone and their temples with the paramagnetic variety. All over Ireland there are many enigmatic round towers standing like obelisks in the landscape, considered by the locals to be ancient sacred monuments. When Callaghan tested these towers, he found to his surprise that even on the plains of central Ireland, they were made of the highly paramagnetic stone found in the mountains.

The old stonemasons who built the ancient cities of Mesopotamia (Babylon),

Egypt, China, South and Central America also used both paramagnetic and diamagnetic limestone in the building of their pyramids and temples. For example, the core blocks of the Great Pyramid in Egypt, each weighing an average of 2.5 tons, originate from local opencast quarries of paramagnetic oolitic stone, whereas the diamagnetic pure limestone blocks that formed the polished casing stones came from quarries on the opposite side of the River Nile. The pink Aswan granite within the Pyramid is generally believed to serve as decoration or strength, but it may also have a symbolic purpose, as Callahan's tests showed it to be the most paramagnetic of all the stones.

Considering there is no clear evidence that the pyramids were originally built as a tomb, Callahan's theories imply that the Egyptians understood the effect of placing paramagnetic granite and oolitic limestone within the insulating diamagnetic pure limestone casings to create some sort of accumulator or battery of cosmic energy drawn into the monument through the capstone. They even had a hieroglyph for white limestone, a rectangle with three lines dividing it into four segments, similar to lines of force.

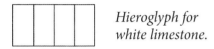

*Hieroglyph for white limestone.*

Significantly, Portland has both types of limestone within its strata, identical to those used to build the pyramids: the shelly oolitic Roach is identical to the core blocks, and the Whitbed or Basebed layers are the same as the outer casings.

The famous dowser Tom Graves also recognised the qualities of oolitic limestone while investigating the prehistoric Rollright Stone Circle in Oxfordshire as part of the Dragon Project. Paul Devereux set up the project in 1977 to investigate claims of strange phenomena at the site, such as balls of light, people receiving electric shocks from the stones and discoveries of ley lines and earth energies. Over a period of 10 years, he used the stone circle as a base for his experiments using a variety of techniques which included sensitive scientific equipment, photography, dowsing and psychic ability.

During this experiment, particularly at dawn and sunset, his equipment captured strange sounds and lights around the weathered oolitic stones. Graves considered that the quartz seeds within this type of stone act as accumulators for a type of static electromagnetic energy generated by water streams beneath. When these seeds become overcharged, the released energy manifests as balls of light.[4] According to Graves' thesis, the great number of flowing subterranean rivers and streams under Portland's oolitic limestone would create a large amount of electromagnetism within its strata. Over the years there have been many reports of strange lights seen around the island; some believe they are mischievous fairies or pixies, even UFOs, but there could be a more scientific explanation.

During the late 1930s in the USA, the exiled Austrian scientist Wilhelm Reich discovered a biologically produced radiation he called 'orgone'.[5] This natural energy, emitted by all living matter, can sometimes take the shape of balls of light. It collects around freshwater lakes and springs and in the upper atmosphere. He even believed that orgone is allied to the concept of cosmological ether of space and the hidden life force that regulates the planet and its weather system. He developed a device called an 'orgone accumulator', a chamber lined with alternating layers of organic and inorganic material to attract and focus this 'life force'. Reich built accumulators large enough to contain a person and claimed noticeable healing results in the cure of mental disorders and cancer. In spite of all the positive results, investigations by the government claimed Reich's accumulators a sham and orgone-energy non-existent. A judge ordered an injunction for all accumulators to be destroyed including all information on orgone energy. Two years later Reich died in prison serving a sentence for contempt of the injunction.

Earth mystery researchers have realised that the prehistoric barrows and earthworks of Wessex and Ireland also have alternating layers of organic earth and inorganic chalk similar to Reich's orgone accumulator – the Boyne Valley mounds of Newgrange and Knowth in Ireland being the best examples.

The surrounding diamagnetic sea provides an insulator for the unique geology of Portland and its cliffs layered with organic diamagnetic and inorganic paramagnetic limestone, creating a large orgone accumulator or battery of natural energy. Portland has additional frictional forces enveloping its shores through the powerful collision of east and west tides off the south coast of the island, called the Portland Race. Furthermore, the constant action of the waves on the highly paramagnetic flint pebbles of Chesil Beach helps to amplify the powerful forces already latent in the island strata.

These theories allow us a deeper insight into the mystery of why those small islands that surround Britain have such a sacred nature. Perhaps the perfect balance of natural energies exists on Portland, as the old islanders were attributed with longevity and good health and the island soil and grass are renowned for their remarkable fertility.

Kings of England also recognised the qualities of Portland stone, including William the Conqueror, the first Norman King of England (1066–1087), who jealously held Portland as part of his royal estates. He transported the fine Whitbed stone to his new capital for the building of the Tower of London, creating his most powerful statement as a new ruler, especially as it was over the site of a ceremonial Druidic mound. The Master Architect Sir Christopher Wren, one of the greatest minds of his day, brought prosperity to the island when he chose the white Portland stone to rebuild London after the Great Fire in 1666. His grand plan was to create a 'shining city of light' to rival Paris and Rome. Amongst many of the buildings constructed with this stone are St Paul's Cathedral, the Houses of Parliament, Bank of England, Mansion House, Banqueting House in Whitehall and the National Gallery, as well as most of the churches in the City of London. Perhaps the great success of this newly built city is in some part due to the energetic qualities or sacred nature of Portland stone.

## Topography

Our ancient ancestors revered their rural surroundings, particularly if the mountains, hills or the shape of an island resembled one of their sacred animals or deities. When viewed from a distance by boat, Portland's unusual shape takes the form of a sphinx or crouched lion. The lion was sacred to many ancient cultures, particularly those of the Middle East, who could have visited Portland as they journeyed along Phoenician trade routes. From the air, the isle looks like the beak of a bird, with Chesil Beach, a bank of pebbles, as its neck. It also resembles a horn jutting out from the mainland into the sea; the Druids may have seen this as symbolic of one of their sacred animals or as a god/goddess figure.

A Portland tradition recalls that the earliest island settlers, called 'the Ancients', built the stone monuments and mounds and sculptured the hills with earthen fortifications. We know very little about the Neolithic and Bronze Age peoples, but recent research from the study of some of their stone circles and mounds reveals they were far from primitive in their understanding of the precise movements of the planets and the stars. The geographical position of Portland, a north–south finger of land projecting into the English Channel, allows uninterrupted views of the rising and setting of the sun and moon into and out of the sea. The Ancients would not have failed to utilise this natural observatory.

The Iron Age peoples enhanced the natural defences of the isle, creating double-banked ditches around the highest ground, now called the Verne. Around AD 500, the Saxons began to farm the fertile soil on the high treeless plateau. They divided the area called by locals 'Tophill' into seven large fields, each incorporating a large number of strips called 'lawns'. The Portland system of land inheritance favoured both sexes of the family and over the years the plots were divided and subdivided so that their descendants found themselves owning almost unworkable small strips of land, most of which were destroyed by later quarrying.

The first settlements began where two or three of these great fields converged; this made the rotational working of the surrounding farmland more convenient. The field divisions between the settlements became the ancient roads, some of which survive today. The Saxons probably created the great ponds fed by the springs on Tophill to provide essential water for the needs of the new villagers. Broad strips of ancient common land bounded the fields and stretched between the settlements. The rocky undercliffs, formed by centuries of cliff erosion as well as stone waste from the quarries, are called the Weares, a Celtic word for 'wild ground'.

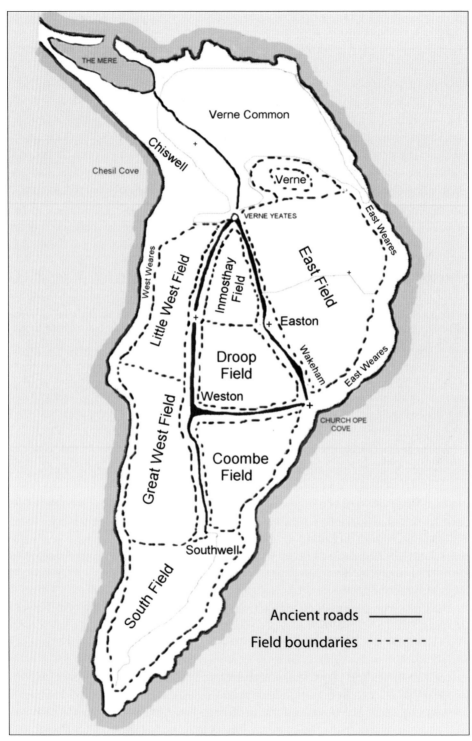

The great fields, villages and ancient roads.

The Saxon settlers also introduced a local governing body known as the Court Leet whose main duty was to oversee the land tenure rights, customs and control of the commons. Its other concern was to guard the commoners' rights against interference from the mainland and the Crown. Unlike other Court Leets in Britain, the continuing sovereign rule and the island's relative isolation from the mainland ensured the Court's survival up to the present day. The Court dealt with a wide range of manorial activities, one of which was the collection of rents from the manor on behalf of the King or Queen. The title given to the person who carried out these activities was 'The Reeve'. Originally the rents paid by each tenant were recorded on a square-sectioned pole about 10 ft long called a Reeve pole or staff. This ancient method of accounting, using cuts and notches, continued up until the nineteenth century.

Before the Victorian period, the Tophill settlements that bounded the great fields with their own ponds grew into villages called Easton, Weston, Wakeham and Southwell. On the north coast below the plateau is an area settled by mariners and fishermen which the locals refer to as 'Underhill'. The oldest of these settlements is Chiswell. Its important location provided a defence against anyone approaching on foot across the long strand of Chesil Beach. The village also served as a port for the Mere, an ancient tidal lagoon used for centuries as a natural harbour. In the twentieth century, the Royal Navy drained the Mere to make way for a naval base, and huge rusting fuel tanks mark the area today. A later harbour east of the Mere, built to ship the vast quantity of stone quarried on the island, resulted in Castletown. The name derives from King Henry VIII's seaside castle built to help defend the nation against French invaders.

Neighbouring Chiswell on the road to Tophill is Fortuneswell, a Victorian village with a high street so steep that in places you are almost level with the chimneys. A further climb takes you up to a sharp bend called Priory and then to the plateau at a roundabout and hotel called The Heights. From here you can enjoy spectacular views over Chesil Beach and the mainland. This large roundabout, which directs you to all parts of the island, has the name of Yeates, an Old English word for 'gap'.

The road heading east goes to the Verne, the highest point on the island and the site of an Iron Age hillfort destroyed during the building of the Victorian Citadel for the defence of England. In 1948 it became a prison and remains so today. The western exit from the roundabout leads on to the ancient road of Wide Street, past the eighteenth century church of St George at Reforne, and then eventually to the village of Weston, which boasts the only Tudor cottage on the island.

Travelling south from Yeates brings you to the central village of Easton with its Edwardian square, and further along as the road starts to widen you enter ancient Wakeham. The old stone cottages on this unusually wide street are good examples of the fine workmanship of the old Portland stonemasons. At the end of the road, opposite the entrance to Pennsylvania Castle, is a thatched cottage, now the Portland Museum. If you turn left there, a narrow lane takes you to the ruins of Rufus Castle, which overlooks the remains of St Andrew's Church, with Church Ope Cove, also called Church Hope Cove, below.

Following the road from Wakeham you eventually pass through the village of Southwell, and from there to the Bill where two lighthouses rise out of the most southerly tip of the island.

Victorian maps show only two main routes through Portland, which the old islanders considered ancient, possibly Roman or even Iron Age (1000–50 BC). One of these routes links the only two landing places on the Island, the Mere and Church Ope Cove.

During the Victorian period, from the viewpoint near Yeates overlooking Chiswell and Fortuneswell, you could still trace the old route from the Mere to Tophill. A faint path gradually ascending from the Mere wound its way along the lower slopes of the Verne behind St John the Baptist Church to a level area behind the Old Portland Arms pub, said to be the site of a Roman camp. As it reached the lower slopes of Tophill, at the bottom of Old Hill Road, the track turned up past the Rectory towards Yeates. From the present roundabout, the route continued along Easton Lane, through the village of Easton along Straits and Wakeham Street to St Andrew's Church, terminating at Church Ope Cove.

The other ancient route, formerly known as Wide Street, began at Yeates and continued through the village of Weston to Southwell.

Before the building of Pennsylvania Castle in 1800 in Wakeham, another ancient track existed between Weston and St Andrew's Church, creating a triangular system of roads. These roads may be older than Roman, as the Latin invaders often laid down their roads on earlier tracks. King Warry refers to the opinion of a travelling antiquarian who describes these well-marked routes as Roman, intended for chariot racing.[6] Roman historians recorded the great effectiveness of the native British war chariots against their armies.

King Warry also mentions that stone circles lay either side of the old route along Easton Lane near the site of the old Saw Mill Tavern. There is a strong possibility that the building of these circles was a deliberate act to mark an already existing Bronze Age track, or the track was a later construction made to pass between the circles to establish a sacred route. King Warry also noted that these circles had some ceremonial or astronomical purpose, as a line drawn between the Mere (the old harbour, now Osprey Quay) and St Andrew's Church at Church Ope Cove passes straight between them. Sadly, the intensive quarrying in Victorian times destroyed many of these monuments and changed this ancient topography forever.

# Chapter 2

# Monuments of the Ancients

Amongst the fields and commons of the high windy plateau, a great number of standing stones and barrows built by 'the Ancients' were still seen and described in the eighteenth and nineteenth centuries by locals and travelling antiquarians. My fascination with the ancient megaliths around Britain and their mysterious builders gave me the incentive to search Portland for any vestiges of these monuments that might have survived quarrying.

After reading all of King Warry's books and other works by antiquarians who visited Portland, it appears that St Andrew's Church at Church Ope Cove was not the only place considered to be sacred on Portland. The area around the Grove before the nineteenth century was rich in so-called Druidical remains, including two stone circles. However, descriptions of these stones given by the old Portlanders indicate that they were more akin to Bronze Age circles found in other areas of Dorset and on Dartmoor in Devon, which date to a thousand years before the Druids. The Druids often utilised these stones for their own religious practices long after the Ancients had abandoned them. In Victorian times, despite the tradition that the Grove was sacred ground, many locals including Elizabeth Pearce avoided the standing stones, based on stories that the Druids performed human sacrifice there.

At the end of Grove Road stands a large foreboding Victorian building made of Portland stone, formerly Portland Prison and now the Young Offenders Institution. In 1847, locals protested at the destruction of the Druid circle to make way for the hastily built prison that was to house the convict workforce brought to the island to build the Breakwater.

King Warry mentions an entry in the diary of Mr W.L. Pearce dating from 1863 that ancient stones were numerous in many parts of the island. He further states that:

> "... certain Druidical Stones were situated in a spot which now forms part
> of the garden in the Grove pertaining to the Prison Governor's house, and

*that when the garden was formed, they were taken and used for ornamental purposes."[1]*

Some locals say the stones were used for a rockery in the Prison Governor's garden, but later removed because of their pagan associations. According to King Warry, remains of another stone circle once stood on the cliffs at the end of Grove Road, part of which had fallen over the edge to the Weares below in late Victorian times.[2]

In 1824, a few years before the building of the prison, the travelling antiquarian Fido Lunettes visited the Grove accompanied by a local surgeon. There he found an ancient British earthwork on the cliffs at the Grove (now destroyed), called Arun's Green, where a local tradition says a great battle took place. Directly below in the Weares they could see the remains of some circles with stones measuring 5–6 ft[2] and a large flat stone held aloft by upright stones called a cromlech or dolmen with a capstone that measured 18 ft long, 6 ft wide and 4 ft thick.[3]

*Sea wall containing large stones at the end of Grove Road.*

Remnants of the Grove monuments may have survived in the sea wall opposite the end of Grove Road, which contains some unusually large weathered stones. Perhaps these were the stones used as rockery in the Prison Governor's garden.

Less than a mile north of the Grove is a freestanding pillar left by quarrymen as a monument or marker called Nicodemus Knob. Its height at 30 ft gives a good indication of the vast amount of stone quarried away to provide the building material for the Verne Citadel and the Breakwater. Its purpose is uncertain; some believe it to be a landmark for ships, while others say it is a boundary marking the eastern end of the commons. Rock columns such as Nicodemus Knob, whether they are natural or man-made, continue to attract the pagan and the 'sensitive' in many places around Britain. The aboriginal natives of many countries around the world also revere these formations. In the work of Professor Callahan, stone towers, obelisks, spires and natural rock pillars act as magnetic antennae because their shape and type of stone attract cosmic forces.[4]

Alternatively, the pillar could mark a place of sanctity as W.L. Pearce mentions that a group of Druidical stones were down in the Weares below Nicodemus Knob.[1] Elizabeth Pearce also refers to these stones in her memoirs (c 1805).[5] While overlooking a gap in the cliff above Nicodemus Knob, she saw the remains of a circle of stones still part-standing that had fallen with the cliff in one of the many landslides.

*Nicodemus Knob.*

I wondered why the Ancients built so many sacred monuments between Nicodemus Knob and the Grove. Elizabeth Pearce may give us a clue to this when she describes a natural phenomenon in the Grove area "… when the moon rises red across St Alban's Head the first rays fall athwart this place".[5] The megalithic priests may have used fixed markers such as stone circles in this area to observe the moon and its 18.6-year cycle. The later Druids probably re-used the circles for a similar purpose. Although 'the Grove' may conjure up images of a double row of trees, it is also a word linked with the moon and used to describe an altar or place of the goddess.

The footpath heading north from Nicodemus Knob, once part of the Admiralty Quarry to Castletown railway, takes you along a shelf beneath the towering cliffs towards the defences of the Verne prison. Here Rodney Legg and a friend had a strange experience.[6] At a point along the path, they heard screaming and wailing as if they were listening to a recording of some gruesome past incident, such as one of the many shipwrecks that have occurred in this area. When visiting the same spot in 2003, I too had an unusual experience. At one point below the cliffs still within view of Nicodemus Knob, I heard shouting, which seemed to come from the sea below, but there was no one there. Is it possible that the shape of the cliffs here act as an amplifier to focus sound from a great distance? Perhaps the paramagnetic qualities of the immense limestone cliffs somehow store sounds from the past, like a tape recorder.

I noticed another curious feature in the area of the Grove while exploring the old piers down in the Weares below the Young Offenders Institution. Looking back at the cliffs, a little further south along the lower footpath, I observed that their natural weathering had created an outline of a giant's head peering down at me. Coincidently it is adjacent to where King Warry saw the half-fallen circle south of the Grove mentioned earlier. I discovered that during the Victorian period this section of cliffs had the name Nicodemus Knowle. In the Grail legends, Nicodemus fashioned a head of Jesus on the day that he had seen the Lord on the cross.

*The head on the cliffs near the Grove.*

In an area now used as playing fields, between the little Catholic church at the Grove and the site of Crown Farm Estate (near the junction of Grove Road and Easton Lane), was a circular ditched enclosure containing standing stones that the Victorians called 'The Frolic'. Lunettes described it as 'two circles of stone one within the other' and believed the site originally covered 4–5 acres. Susann Palmer, a Portland archaeologist, says they were still standing in the early twentieth century and may have formed part of a ritual landscape with the circle nearer the cliffs, and adds that some of the stones may have found their way into the walls of the nearby cottages.[7]

North along Easton Lane is a castled Victorian building called the Drill Hall, used by the Portland Volunteer Artillery Brigade in 1868. Across the road from here, Elizabeth Pearce recorded seeing another group of ancient standing stones.

The Saw Mill circles mentioned earlier were situated just north of the Drill Hall, where there used to be a public house called the Saw Mill Tavern. In the nineteenth century, locals observed two stone circles close to the Tavern either side of the old road. One stood behind the Tavern and the other on the verge of the quarry opposite.[2]

While investigating the area along Easton Lane near the site of the Saw Mill Tavern, I noticed ancient weathered stones set into the walls either side of the road that I felt sure were the megaliths from these circles. Some of the stones have the same shape and characteristic weathering as the megaliths on Dartmoor. More of these old stones are in a wall on the road behind the Heights Hotel. Why they have been set into the walls is a mystery. Possibly Elizabeth Pearce provides the reason, when she mentions that the locals or quarrymen were superstitious of these stones. They probably refused to break them up for fear of being cursed, and decided to preserve them close to where they were removed.

*Weathered megaliths near the site of Saw Mill Tavern, Easton Lane.*

Elizabeth Pearce also mentions stone rows on the southern part of the island, particularly towards the Bill.[6] A pair of stones marked on old maps in a field in Southwell and another pair in the ancient strip fields south of the village may have been part of this stone row.

On the east coast, a little south of the village of Southwell, is a small inlet bearing the name Longstone Ope, so called from a local tradition that a great

*Old stones behind the Heights Hotel.*

fallen monolith once lay in the area. The purpose of these tall single standing stones is still a mystery, but the situation of this particular stone on Portland near the coast may indicate its function as a marker for ancient mariners.

Another observation I made was that the Saw Mill circles and the circle destroyed in the Prison Governor's garden lay on a geological fault between the Purbeck Beds and the Portland Stone series. Earth mystery researchers have discovered that many stone circles are close to fault lines. When seismic stress or earth movement takes place, the extreme pressure placed on the faults between the meetings of two different types of rock creates a subtle form of electricity that radiates upwards to the nearest site of discharge. A standing stone or a group of them would make a perfect antenna to store or release this electricity.

As mentioned in the Introduction, during the late 1970s, as part of the Dragon Project, Paul Devereux and a team of scientists performed incredible research using sophisticated monitors at the Rollright Stones in Oxfordshire, which was sited near a major fault line. Particularly at dawn and sunset, their meters showed a 'shear force' exerting itself on the fault line whenever the sun or moon crossed the horizon, creating a subtle energy on the ground like a tidal pull. For what purpose the Ancients may have utilised this energy is still a mystery.

Having at least six stone circles within a mile of each other is evidence that the megalithic priests considered Portland to be a sacred island. Perhaps they built these circles as instruments to release seismic forces to help stabilise the strata of the island, or maybe they regarded this long slender finger of land thrust out into the sea as an ideal solar and lunar observatory. One thing is certain; the megalithic priests were obsessed with accurately marking events such as the luna standstill and the solstices all over Europe with stones and earth mounds. Before the destruction of Tophill, from the elevated area around the Saw Mill Tavern where the circles once stood there would have been unobstructed views of the horizon around the island, including down to the Bill. Because the accuracy of plotting the sun's movements, particularly at sunrise and sunset, was paramount to the megalithic priests, Portland must have been the ideal place to observe the cycles of the sun and moon and movements of the stars. These priests were also keen observers of the planet Venus, and King Warry cites Thomas Hardy as stating "… tradition urged that a temple to Venus once stood at the top of the Roman road leading up into the isle".[8] Was this a temple of the goddess, or a stone observatory for monitoring the planet?

# A Burial Place of Kings

Before the interior quarrying of the island, Portland had a large number of burial mounds scattered around the island, some recorded by Lunettes and King Warry, whilst others are now only a memory kept alive by folklore and place names. Two of the largest mounds were long barrows, possibly dating from the Neolithic period (c 4000 BC). The names Rough Barrow and Barrow Hill may indicate later round barrows and 'cist burials' (stone coffins) from the Bronze Age (2300–1000 BC). Celtic Iron Age and Roman burials from 1000 BC to AD 350 were also numerous on the island.

King Barrow Quarry near Yeates takes its name from a great Neolithic mound, the possible burial place of a king. Another long barrow or 'cursus', recorded by Elizabeth Pearce, stood on the Verne Common, today a naval cemetery near Castletown. King Warry also mentions that two uprights and a table-like slab stood near Castletown and were still standing about 1860. A large Bronze Age cemetery between Southwell and the Bill contained up to 200 burials, and hundreds of carved stone-lidded sarcophagi have been found in areas such as the Grove, Southwell, the Verne and on the Verne Common.

Behind a building, formerly the Driftwood Gallery, in Chiswell is the only surviving burial mound on the island, now in the garden of a private house. Its name is Mound Oel or Owl, although some authorities refer to it as Mount Howle. According to one story a Viking leader is buried here; others

*Mound Owl (Oel) in Chiswell.*

claim it is the grave of two Saxon Princes killed in a battle with the Danes.[9] In Cumbria, 'howe' means 'burial place', although the name may also be a corruption of Howel, the last British Prince of Cornwall, killed in battle with Athelstan, Saxon King of Wessex, in the tenth century. King Warry believed that Athelstan built the first stone church on Portland.

Another burial mound known as Bran's Barrow became a landmark for ships centuries ago, situated in the valley called Branscombe leading down to Chiswell. The name Bran also occurs in other neighbouring places such as Branscombe Hill between Southwell and the Bill and Bran's Point on the coast of Dorset opposite Portland.[1] Bran must have been an important man to have such a large burial mound and so many places named after him; perhaps he was a local king? There is a Bran recorded in ancient British history as the father of the Welsh hero Caractacus, famous for resisting the Romans.[10] Arthurian romances refer to Bran as the Grail or Fisher King whose head, according to legend, was buried in the White Mound as protection against invasion and plague. The White Mound was a Druidical ceremonial site over which William the Conqueror built the Tower of London using Portland stone.[11] Legend says King Arthur removed the head of Bran for fear that the Saxons would destroy this potent symbol of protection. Bran was also the name of the last Arch Druid during the period of the Roman invasions who peaceably converted many pagans to Christianity in Wales.[12]

Archaeological excavations indicate that Dorset was one of the last frontiers against the Saxons during the time of Arthur around AD 520. Did Arthur bring the head to Portland, 'the fortress island', for safekeeping, or was the headless body of Bran buried here in a prominent barrow overlooking the English Channel to protect Britain? The early Welsh manuscripts refer to the graves of the British heroes and kings, except for Bran. The site of his grave has always remained a mystery. Unfortunately, any Dark Age records of Dorset seem to have been destroyed or deliberately erased by the Saxons, except for the oral traditions and place names. One of the most famous of Dorset traditions is that Arthur fought his greatest battle against the Saxons at Badbury Rings, 25 miles north-east of Portland.

There is no trace today of the other barrows recorded, such as Row Barrow, where 20 skeletons in a crouching position were unearthed near the Bill. Neither is there any trace of mounds on Barrow Hill near Southwell, Round Barrow and the mound still remembered by locals behind the old fishermen's cottages near Brandy Row. It is interesting that the Ancients built most of the mounds on the western side of the island facing the setting sun, as earlier cultures believed souls travelled in this direction on their journey to the realms of the dead.

# Sacred Waters

Natural springs were sacred places long before man ever erected a stone. Their constant trickle through rocks and stones in the most unexpected places continues to thwart the ravages of time. The sacred waters of Portland determined the place of settlements and gave life to its people. Some of the springs were made into ponds, such as those at Easton (now the Edwardian Square), Weston (on the green) and Wakeham (Pound Piece). Other springs became drinking wells. Those that never ran dry even in the worst of droughts were considered holy; the Ancients would say that even when mother earth is dry and suffering she could still provide her life-giving essence.

The Celts believed that wells were the haunt of spirits, to be honoured and nurtured with offerings; the elemental guardians would then provide good health and fortune, hence the name wishing well. There are hundreds of famous wells around the country where healing has taken place, in many cases documented. I discovered that many of the most renowned healing wells are those that face the eastern sunrise. In Dorset, there are several wells known to relieve eye complaints and the tradition is to bathe in them as the early morning sun casts its first rays upon the water. There may be some truth to this ancient practice as modern research has discovered that ozone is released when the first rays of the sun illuminate the water. Ozone therapy is used to oxygenate the human body to help fight disease. Other healing qualities, besides the mineral content, come from the natural energies of the rocks and the soil absorbed in the water beneath the earth. This is released when the water reaches the surface air. Is it any wonder our ancient ancestors revered natural springs?

A path along the West Weares known as Hiram's Walk takes you past beach huts to Jacob's Well, formerly Silver Well. Long ago, this ancient spring, though facing west, provided safe drinking water up until the twentieth century when other wells became contaminated. The name Silver Well may refer to the ancient tradition of offering silver coins or charms for good health and fortune. Silver may also refer to the worship of the moon whose silvery reflective rays on the waters of a holy well induce

*Jacob's Well.*

oracular experiences.

Hiram Otter, a quarryman of great stature with a vast knowledge of Portland folklore, built the footpath along the West Weares in the 1880s. He painted and carved religious texts on the rocks either side of the path that takes you to a cove he christened Hallelujah Bay. It was at this time that he renamed the spring Jacob's Well. Unfortunately most of the inscriptions are no longer visible due to erosion, except for the single word 'Jessu', now defaced, on one of the rocks. Another well lies near the sculptured grass terraces just before the huts in Chesil Cove.

Some of the old wells survive on Portland, while the memories of others are recalled in the place names of Southwell, Maidenwell and Fortuneswell. The little square at the foot of the High Street below Fortuneswell, now a triangular parking area, is marked on early maps as the site of a well. There is also a well in the garden of a house further up the High Street. Maybe one of these wells gave its name to the area of Maidenwell.

The village of Fortuneswell also derived its name from a famous watering place, now filled in and located behind the bus shelter at the top of the High Street. This spring, formerly known as St Mary's Well, had a reputation for

*Culverwell.*

never drying up even in the driest of summers. A drawing by Swiss artist S. Grim sketched in 1790 can be found in Stuart Morris's book *Portland, An Illustrated History*, depicting women washing clothes at the well.[16]

Marked on early maps of Portland, to the south of St George's Church on the east side of the road, is Merry Well. Sadly, like so many of Portland's ancient sacred sites, it is no longer visible.

My favourite well or spring is set amongst the ancient strip fields between Southwell and the Bill, called Culverwell. Still visible amongst the tangle of bushes, this well faces east and therefore has the power to heal. Ancient Whitbed stones line the circumference of the well and large shelly pillars of Roach lie across the clear waters. This method of construction is similar to St Mary's Well; its purpose is to allow visitors to sit and collect water or wash their clothes (as shown in the drawing by Grim[9]). The spring is abundant with wild watercress during summer and feeds a stream that leads to a waterfall cascading over the cliffs. Although the site has no recorded history, its proximity to the Mesolithic site close by suggests its use from the earliest period of settlement in Dorset.[7] Local author Penny Protheroe refers to the well as a place of secret beauty.[13]

Among the huts at Church Ope Cove, next to the water tap, is another enclosed spring with ancient stones. The triangular green below St Andrew's Avalanche Church in Southwell once housed a well that gave the village its name.

*Well at Church Ope Cove.*

# Chapter 3

# A Hallowed Centre and Lost Lands

*"I'm sure our island could tell the most wondrous tales, if it could speak. Castles and churches, roads and piers all nearly vanished! And Roman and Danish earthworks, circles and barrows, before ever castle or church was thought of, the Parson says. Is it any wonder that Kings came here, and called it their own, and made it one of their homes? Is it any wonder that places with no such past fail to understand us?"*

(King Warry)[1]

My fascination with folklore and its hidden meanings prompted me to explore whether there is any symbolic truth to the myths attached to the landscape features on Portland.

King Warry refers to the area surrounding Rufus Castle and the ancient church of St Andrew as 'God's Acre', once the centre of the island before a landslip. This hallowed centre, steeped in myth and legend, was the perfect place to begin.

Set upon a levelled area above an inlet called Church Ope Cove is St Andrew's Church, now a romantic ruin residing in a most picturesque part of the island. It was here in the Cove, according to locals, that the first recorded Viking raid took place in Britain. *The Anglo-Saxon Chronicle* refers to the raid on Portland by Northmen as early as AD 787:

*"This year King Bertric took Edburga the daughter of Offa to wife. And in his days came first three ships of the Northmen from the land of robbers. The reeve then rode thereto, and would drive them to the king's town [Dorchester]; for he knew not what they were; and there was he slain. These were the first ships of the Danish men that sought the land of the English nation."[2]*

The *Chronicle* seems to imply that the Northmen were Danes; however, historical experts are divided as to their identity. One theory says they were 'men from the north', ancestors of the Normans who later conquered England; another believes they were a branch of the Vikings from Scandinavia, while others write that they arrived from 'Haeretha-land', also known as Jutland, an early name for a region of Denmark[3], a country that I later found to have substantial links with Portland.

It seems strange that these Northmen, whoever they were, should make Portland their first point of landing on British shores, and even more curious is why they chose Church Ope Cove. If they sailed from the east, then surely the old Dorset ports of Hengistbury Head near Christchurch, Poole Harbour or even Weymouth, opposite Portland, would have provided better pickings for the raiders.

According to local history, the Normans later built a castle here to defend this vulnerable cove; however, a mystery surrounds even this building and its origins.

## Rufus Castle

Rufus Castle, also known as Bow and Arrow Castle, is precariously perched upon a high rock platform overlooking St Andrew's Church and Church Ope Cove. Its shape, an irregular pentagon, is most unusual and the only one of its kind in Britain. The castle is a credit to the stonemasons who fashioned the walls in stone without mortar in the cyclopean way of building, more common to the prehistoric temples of Europe than a supposed Norman castle in England. John Hutchins, a sixteenth century antiquarian, wrote "but little mortar has been used in the construction of the walls which are roughly built of native ashlar".[4] Without mortar, there is no organic material to use for carbon dating the building, leaving experts with only architectural clues to date its precise origins. The mortar seen today is a result of past and present restoration.

According to the information leaflet obtained from the Portland Museum, William Rufus, son of William the Conqueror, constructed the castle probably around AD 1100:

> "William Rufus II, the Conqueror's son, introduced a local annual tax to raise 14 pounds 14 shillings and 3 pennies yearly to help pay for the castle, but when completed he decided to maintain the tax for other purposes and it wasn't until 1935 that the last payment was handed over to the Crown."[5]

Local history states that around 1140 the castle suffered great damage during the ongoing feud between Empress Matilda and King Steven. In 1258, Richard

*Rufus Castle.*

de Clare, Duke of Gloucester, acquired the Isle of Portland from the Benedictine monks of the Church of St Swithun in Winchester, owners of the isle from 1052. Through this acquisition, the Duke became keeper of the castle and obtained a building licence through royal consent allowing him to strengthen the fabric of the building.

Around 1450 another rebuilding took place, possibly due to attacks by the French;

much of the ruined castle we see today probably dates from this period. In 1800, King George III handed over the castle and its lands to John Penn who proceeded to build himself a Gothic home designed by James Wyatt on a sycamore-wooded platform of land nearby. He named his marine mansion Pennsylvania Castle after

*Cyclopean walls.*

his grandfather William Penn, the founder of the state of Pennsylvania in the USA. After the Second World War, a part of the grounds including the ruined castle was sold and remains in private hands today.

In 2004, I attended a charity fete in the grounds of the castle, giving me the opportunity to admire the extraordinary masonry for myself. As I wandered around the garden, I noticed some old stone steps leading down towards the old church. The size and age of the weathered steps made me wonder if they are the ones that Elizabeth Pearce used to run up and down, referred to in *Old Portland*.[7] They seem to have a deeper cut than ordinary steps, as if designed for people with very long legs! Francis Grose[6] and Fido Lunettes mentions there were 50 steps in all.

King Warry refers to an old Portland tradition that Rufus Castle once stood at the centre of the island:

*"They told me that Rufus had built Bow & Arrow Castle in the middle of the island but other Kings had also favoured the Isle in earlier days. They said a terrific storm – an undersea earthquake many thought – had occurred, which caused a terrible subsidence with the land sliding into the sea as far as the Shambles, which were previously butchers' shops. People thought the whole island was sinking into the sea. Bow & Arrow Castle had not been left, however, close to the cliff edge as at present, for the field on the seaward side of the castle, marked in John Speed's map, was still in existence in the eighteenth century, and Grandmother remembered running and playing there as a very young girl."[1]*

The Shambles is now a shallow bank of sand 4 miles out to sea east of the Bill where there was once an anchored light ship before the present navigation buoy.

Evidence of coastal erosion around the castle can be found not only from John Speed's map which shows a field in front of the castle around 1500, but also by the field name that still adjoins the castle – Castle Heys. The name could refer to an earlier enclosure or a bailey that once existed around the castle, typical of Norman motte and bailey fortifications from the time of Rufus. Alternatively, Castle Heys may refer to the earthworks of an older castle favoured by earlier kings, as King Warry suggests. She states:

*"In 1579 Bow and Arrow Castle stood in the midst of a field, and a moat extending from the castle sea-ward was still in existence."[7]*

An earlier or alternative name for Rufus Castle is Giant's Castle, the former name of the nearby Alessandra Hotel. There are many sacred hills around the West Country with folklore stories of giants. The most common tales are those that refer to contests or games such as quoits played from hilltops.

# Lost Lands

The loss of several square miles of Portland was such a colossal disaster that there must have been some record of this event, even a date, but the *Chronicles* are silent. My only option was to research the old Portland traditions.

Gathering dust in the basement of a local museum I found an unpublished work by King Warry entitled *The High Place*. This fascinating hand-typed account of Portland traditions refers to the area around Rufus Castle and Pennsylvania Castle as a sacred site of ceremony from ancient times called the 'High Place'. I also found further details of the legendary landslip, including the actual date the event took place.

*"Roughly this place [High Place] is still central as regards North and South, though it ceased to be equidistant between East and West after the great cataclysm about 1100 AD, when the under-sea earthquake which wrought havoc in the Channel Isles – fortunately confined to a small place – found its vibrations felt on the opposite shore, and caused the disappearance of half of Portland on the south east. Happening at night, the terrors were thereby doubled; and as late as the early nineteenth century the terrible havoc wrought, and the consequent fears of the islanders, remained an often-told tale."*[8]

After reading this account, I decided to research for any further documented evidence in support of this calamity. Finding recorded events from this period proved difficult as so much of the history has been lost or destroyed. However, in *The Anglo-Saxon Chronicle* there is a recorded event that took place on the 11th of November (Martinmas) in AD 1099:

*"… on the festival of St. Martin, the sea-flood sprung up to such a height, and did so much harm, as no man remembered that it ever did before. And this was the first day of the new moon."*[2, 9]

*The Chronicle of Florence of Worcester* records:

*"On the third of the Nones of November [1099] the sea overflowed the shore, destroying towns and drowning many persons and innumerable oxen and sheep."*[10]

Other information from this period is in the form of legends and traditions and deserves to be included as all have some basis in truth and may add weight to the documented evidence already uncovered. According to John Stow's *Chronicles of England* (1580), the great tide of 1099 caused a major catastrophe when:

*"The sea brake in over the banks of the Thames and other ryvers, drowning many towns and much people, with innumerable numbers of oxen and sheepe."*[11]

The Goodwin Sands are a series of sand banks 11 miles long and 6 miles across which lie 6 miles off Deal rounding the North Foreland in the English Channel and for centuries this area has been a graveyard of ships. Traditionally, the Sands were once a fertile low-lying isle called Lomea, belonging to Godwin, Earl of Wessex, Britain's most powerful nobleman during the reign of Edward the Confessor (1042–1066). A great storm in the late eleventh century submerged Lomea and thousands drowned as far south as Kent.[12] The 1099 undersea earthquake may, as King Warry suggests, have been centred near the Channel Islands, as a flood also affected the Dutch coastal areas and as far away as the Scilly Isles.

Lethowsow was the Cornish name given to a lost land between western Cornwall and the present-day Scilly Isles; some romantic poets called it Lyonnesse. There is an old Cornish tradition that a tidal wave covered Lethowsow around this time (eleventh century), leaving only its peaks to become the Scilly Islands. Lord Trevelyan on his white steed was the last man to reach the coast of Cornwall alive and the Trevelyan family still depict on their coat of arms the white horse emerging from the sea.[13] Sonar readings have shown man-made walls and dwellings under the sea off the coast of Land's End.

The Venerable Bede (AD 672–735) was a Northumbrian monk who wrote

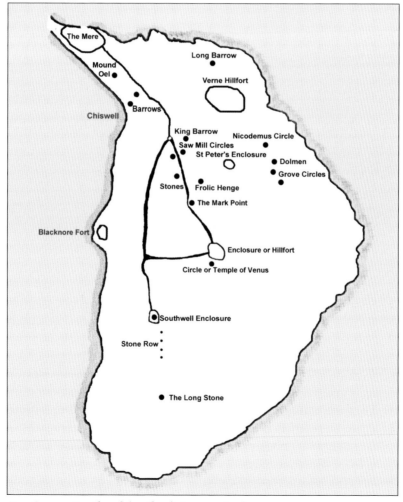

*Pre-Saxon Portland (author's impression).*

many books, including a report on natural phenomena called *De rerum natura*. In this book he describes the dimensions of the Isle of Wight as 30 miles wide. Either his measurements are widely inaccurate or a third of the island has disappeared, for today it stands only 20 miles wide. There is an Isle of Wight legend that tells of the flooding of Brading harbour and the city of Wolverton.[14] On the north coast of the island the low tide reveals prehistoric tracks and a Roman Villa, proof that sea levels changed after the Roman period.[15]

I discovered the coastline of Portland has also changed during the past 500 years. In 1666, the year of the Great Fire of London, landslips destroyed roads and a pier north of the Grove. In 1754, 50 yards of Portland coastline was lost in a landslip[13]; perhaps the large amount of stone quarried on the isle around this time weakened the plateau. Portland is naturally unstable and vulnerable to slippage because the limestone beds lie on top of Kimmeridge Sand; even the most minor of tremors could devastate the island today. I wonder just how many sacred sites such as stone circles and burial mounds disappeared in the Portland landslip of AD 1099? In other parts of Britain it is very rare to find stone circles so near the sea, as the original builders would not risk their destruction from landslips. When the Saxons arrived on the island the circles at the Grove were much further inland, and the area around St Andrew's Church and Rufus Castle were, as the legends say, at the centre of the island.

## St Andrew's Church

From the viewing platform below the castle, a path with steps leads down to Church Ope Cove. Near the bottom of this path, old stone steps ascend to the ruins of St Andrew's Church. The roofless low walls are all that remain of the oldest and probably the only church on the island before the building of St George's Church.

In the 1970s, archaeological excavations of the site revealed Romano-British pottery and an Iron Age coin found in what might be Saxon foundations under the footings of an impressive Norman church. Although there is only fragmentary evidence of a Saxon church, ancient documents might provide further clues that a church once stood on this site before the Norman invasion.

The Anglo-Saxon *Winchester Chronicle* states that Edward the Confessor bestowed Portland upon the Benedictine monks of St Swithun in Winchester in 1042.[16] This transaction took place out of remorse for falsely accusing his own mother Emma of having an affair with Alwyn, the Bishop of Winchester. She proved her innocence by performing the 'Ordeal' of walking across red-hot ploughshares on a pavement within the nave of the city's cathedral.[17, 18] Godwin, father-in-law of Edward the Confessor, was incensed by the Roman ecclesiastical influence on the King and was furious when Edward handed

*The ruins of St Andrew's Church at Church Ope Cove.*

Royal Portland to the Benedictine Order. When Godwin returned from exile in 1051, he wrought revenge by invading Portland and destroying the monks' island sanctuaries and probably the Saxon church.

In *The High Place* King Warry refers to oral traditions of Portland that claim earlier buildings may have existed on the site of old St Andrew's Church: "… a vague story points to a Temple of Venus having occupied the site in pre-Christian days". King Warry believes that before the building of a Saxon Christian church, the occupation of the site may have begun with a prehistoric stone circle or possibly a defensive enclosure, replaced by a Roman temple and later supplanted by a primitive British shrine.[8] If this tradition is true, the temple of Venus may have been either a Romano-British shrine dedicated to the Roman goddess or a stone circle used as an observatory to mark the rising of the 'star' or planet Venus. Such observations have been found elsewhere. For example on the Isle of Anglesey there is a prehistoric stone-chambered barrow built *c* 3500 BC called Bryn Celli Ddu. Latest research reveals that the purpose of this ancient stone temple was to observe not just the cycle of the sun, but also the movement of the star Venus.[19]

Worship often continues at prehistoric circles and earthen enclosures long after the race who built them disappeared, albeit in another form. For example, there is a Norman church built inside a prehistoric henge at Knowlton, near

Wimborne. Portland had a large number of prehistoric monuments, so it is possible that St Andrew's Church replaced a Druidical or prehistoric religious centre.

The governing Benedictine monks formerly of St Swithun's at Winchester built a new church over the earlier Saxon foundations in AD 1100, probably because the earlier building was finally destroyed by the undersea earthquake in November 1099. The building, which included a lantern tower, had stonework of considerable beauty and importance, which Robert Pearce states was Caen stone from France and not Portland stone.[20] This seemed extraordinary to me as they had a vast quantity of excellent building stone in the vicinity. Perhaps the Norman Benedictine monks of Winchester built with Caen limestone to make a statement of their power over the English. Today, remnants of this church are in the garden of the local museum.

Raids by the French in 1339 and in 1404 severely damaged the Norman church, forcing reconstruction in 1475. During this period, the medieval stonemasons built a bell tower separated from the body of the church by 3 ft of space, and this stood as late as 1772. This unusual method of building a freestanding tower, also seen at Wimborne Minster in Dorset, was more typical of the Saxons. Robert Pearce also mentions this and adds, "It seemed, however, to serve no purpose, for we learn there were no bells in it".[20]

The new church was inferior in construction and style to the previous Norman church, probably due to the economic decline of the island caused by French raids and the catastrophic effects of the Black Death. By 1753, the fabric was in a seriously decayed state and the church was becoming too small for the growing congregation; in addition, the cliffs nearby were eroding rapidly, threatening its safety. Consequently, the islanders reluctantly decided to abandon the church altogether, agreeing to build a larger place of worship elsewhere – on a piece of common ground in the more accessible location of Weston Road, formerly Wide Street. Eventually St George's Church opened to the congregation in 1765.

Over time, the old stones of St Andrew's became a source of free stone for the construction of new buildings, leaving us with the ruin we see today. Furthermore, much of the graveyard as well as some infamous graves were lost to cliff erosion. According to King Warry, King Ethelred (AD 979–1016) had his stillborn twin daughters buried in the churchyard; their grave was still in existence before 1790. Elizabeth Pearce as a child remembers seeing this grave marked by a cross before it was carried away by a landslide.[1] If this is true, then it is certain that King Ethelred lived in the Saxon castle that preceded Rufus Castle.

An amusing piece of folklore relates to St Andrew's Church. When Christianity arrived in Portland, the local stonemasons were said to have erected the bell tower first because they feared the Pixies or 'Pexies' would move the foundations overnight. They erected a wooden frame, hoisted the bell and rang it continually to ward off the elementals, who detested such noise; locals saw the Pixies leaving the island across Chesil Beach to find a new home on the mainland.[21] The Mermaid Inn, a few doors up from the museum, is so named after a most unusual event that apparently took place in Church Ope Cove. A creature, half human half fish, was witnessed on the rocks below by some of the congregation on their way to a service at St Andrew's Church. Other versions suggest that locals carried the mermaid up to the church where she died at noon,[22] probably burying her in the churchyard.

I remember that my first experience of St Andrew's Church was standing amongst the old graves and sensing its sacred atmosphere. I believe that when our outer focus balances and blends with our inner focus, we can appreciate a sense of sacredness. Often people find inspiration to greater things when they connect with the countryside and its special locations. Within our landscape are sacred centres of power, marked by our prehistoric ancestors who had a great understanding of and sensitivity to this natural energy. The strong magnetic fields recorded at many of these sites have a subliminal effect on the senses; this may lead to visions or dreams for those who are sensitive.

After this experience, I had a hunch to examine detailed maps of Portland and soon discovered a mysterious plan centred on St Andrew's Church.

# Chapter 4

# Discovery of the Divine Circles: The Invisible Pattern

So why was the site of St Andrew's Church the chosen centre for worship over many centuries, despite its inaccessibility for most of the islanders, particularly those living in Chiswell? Surely it would have been more suitable to build a place of worship north of Easton in a more central position for the population? However, it appears that the site itself may have some religious significance and, as King Warry mentions, it was once at the centre of the island before the great undersea earthquake.

After reading many books on the religious practices of the Celts and Saxons, I discovered they revered the geographical centre of their Kingdom. John Michell writes that "... the powers of ancient rulers emanated from the ritual centre of the tribal territory".[1] In other words, from a ritual or sacred centre, the King and his geomancers would survey the realm and divide it in accordance with the harmony and balance of the cosmos. According to Michell, such sacred centres were the governing points of many of the various islands around Britain such as the Faroes, Shetlands, Orkney and the Isle of Man. These islands were all sacred to the Celtic Druids and the Norsemen. After aligning their sites to the ritual centre or omphalos, surveyors would build temples, churches, political and military buildings on an esoteric foundation plan of sacred geometry using straight lines, circles and pentagrams.

With this in mind, I decided to see how central St Andrew's Church was on a large-scale map of Portland.

## The Circle of St Andrew

I started by placing a compass with the point on St Andrew's Church and the pencil on the Bill at the southern tip of the island. The completed circle passes straight through Portland Castle built in 1520 by King Henry VIII on the very northern tip of the island, proving that St Andrew's is indeed central in a north–south direction. I then wondered if there was an inner circle, so I reduced the compass' size, keeping the centre as before, but placing the pencil on St George's Church. Incredibly, this circle passed exactly through St Andrew's Avalanche Church in the village of Southwell and the Roman Catholic Church at the Grove dedicated to Our Lady and St Andrew. Although there are other 'rings of sites' in other areas of Britain, I considered this one remarkable because it connects three churches dedicated to St Andrew.

From an early age, I had a great passion for geography, prehistoric sites and ancient mysteries. This combination of interests found personal fulfilment in another of John Michell's books, *The New View Over Atlantis*, first published in

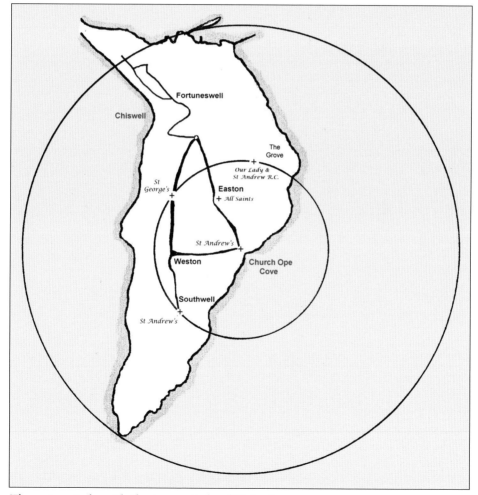

*The outer circle with the inner circle of St Andrew.*

1969.[2] After reading this fascinating book, I joined with others in the popular pastime of ley hunting, a practice first popularised by Alfred Watkins in the 1920s.[3] Leys are alignments of churches drawn on a map that also include ancient sites such as hillforts, burial mounds and holy wells. Today this subject is gathering popularity and is widely published. During my own research of this phenomenon, I also found that some ancient sites lie on the circumference of circles, such as the St Andrew circle I had just discovered.

A detailed study of the St Andrew circle using larger-scale maps indicated that the centre point of the circle needed positioning at the far eastern end of the old church for the outer circle to pass through the other churches. This key point marks the site where the sacred high altar once stood. I also discovered that the distance from this centre to the three churches is approximately 0.85 of a mile .

In addition to the three churches, another building of note lies upon the circle, the unusual Victorian turreted building near Easton called the Drill Hall; over 100 yards of footpath leading from here to St George's coincides with the arc of the circle. I was convinced that the placement of these buildings was intentional rather than just a random accident, as the odds of this happening by chance are very slim.

What is also rather mysterious is that the ruined church, placed at the centre of the circle, is on a ledge halfway down a cliff and not visible to any of the other churches. I wondered if the Portlanders deliberately planned to build their new religious houses the same distance from the old mother church to honour the old ritual centre or omphalos. The circle is a figure of infinity having no end or beginning. In occult magic, a circle is a means of protection to defend a person or place from negative forces. One of the most important and powerful symbols in sacred geometry and Freemasonry is a point within a circle. The point represents the centre of the universe around which everything revolves. The word 'geometry' literally means measuring the Earth. Nigel Pennick described geometry as underlying

> *"... the structure of all things – from the galaxies to molecules. Each time a geometrical form is created, an expression of this universal oneness is made … sacred geometry is responsible for the feeling of awe generated by a Gothic cathedral as well as for the 'rightness' of a Georgian drawing room."[4]*

The architects and builders of the great European medieval cathedrals incorporated sacred geometry in their designs.

The Old Testament in the Bible contains detailed descriptions of buildings constructed with measurements given directly by God, such as Solomon's Temple in Jerusalem. Hiram Abif, the Phoenician architect of Solomon's Temple, incorporated the secrets of the 'divine proportions' into his construction. Ancient civilisations such as Egypt and Greece understood this proportion and incorporated it into the construction of their temples. This ancient measure, called the golden section, is 1.618 of any given length. The principle of this is dividing a line into unequal parts in such a way that the ratio of the whole to the longer part equals the ratio of the longer part to the shorter.

Authors on this subject suggest that this knowledge continued underground from ancient times through generations of stonemasons, Guilds, Freemasons, the Knights Templars and secret societies such as the Rosicrucians. Today this code is still contained in the fabric of churches and temples around the world.

The question remains, does the invisible circle I found on Portland adhere to this secret code and therefore would its origins lie in modern times or in a period long forgotten? To answer these questions I first had to determine whether the three other churches on the circle are also places of significance like the old ruin of St Andrew's.

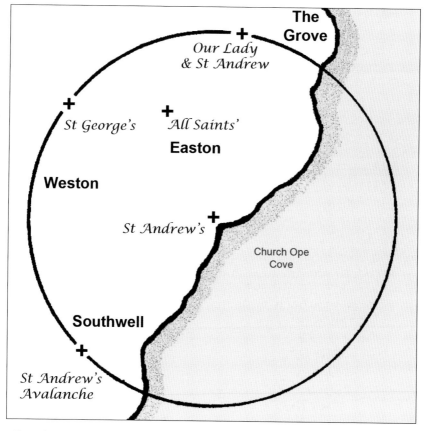

*Churches on the circle of St Andrew.*

## St Andrew's Avalanche Church, Southwell

The ancient village of Southwell, the most southerly settlement on Portland, lies in a shallow valley sheltered by low hills on three sides with plenty of fresh water from nearby streams, an ideal site for early settlers. The church, built in 1879, commemorates the brave locals who, at great risk to themselves, saved the lives of 12 crewmembers of the ships *Avalanche* and *Forest* when they collided southwest of the Bill. The site of the church, standing upon a raised knoll or mound, may have been an earlier sacred site, as a long-standing tradition refers to an ancient enclosure existing at Southwell.[5]

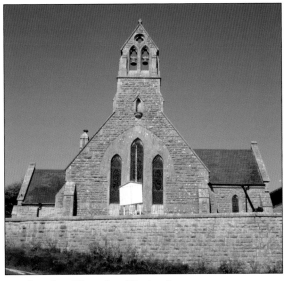

*Avalanche Church of St Andrew.*

Archaeological finds in the vicinity date back to the Bronze and Iron Ages. Pieces of tessellated pavement, allegedly found by locals near the church, might indicate the site of a Romano-British temple. A nearby spring fed a well on the triangular green below the church to supply this settlement, giving the village its name. I noticed that the axis of the church is unusually oriented to the north-west instead of east. After checking with the compass and detailed maps of the island, I discovered that the axis of the church points precisely towards St Andrew's at Church Ope Cove. I wondered if the builders of this church were giving us a clue to its secret relationship with the old mother church.

As previously mentioned, the church stands on a knoll close to a well within a possible circular settlement. Such high places were sacred to the Ancients, where they would have performed open-air seasonal ceremonies; later they became sites of temples built of wood or stone.

## St George's Church, Reforne

Continuing clockwise, the next church on the circle is St George's, built in 1754 and considered the most impressive Georgian building in Dorset. After the closure of St Andrew's at Church Ope Cove, Reforne was the new site chosen for the place of worship, a location more central for the congregation. The Webb map of 1800 in Weymouth library shows the church positioned in the middle of ancient Wide Street.

*St George's Church.*

The church's architect, Thomas Gilbert, was a Master Builder and a Portlander whose roots on the island go back 500 years. He designed the new church in the classical Georgian style to a cruciform plan, including a central saucer dome and a western cupola tower. The tower is similar in design to that of St Paul's Cathedral built by Sir Christopher Wren. Members of the local Methodist movement helped to build the church, taking some 12 years to complete it. The splendid box pews still survive today due to the customs of the island: shared inheritance of land and property, including freehold rights to the pews. Another unique custom once practised in this church was the conveyance of property, known as Church Gift, whereby the two parties involved would attend the church to sign a contract in the presence of two witnesses.

During the Victorian period, modernisation of the interior took place including the rearrangement of the pews. Sadly, by the beginning of the twentieth century, the church was in desperate need of repair and restoration, as many of the part-owners of the pews were long gone from the island, and the congregation started to decrease. The church closed in preference to the churches of St John the Baptist in Fortuneswell, built in 1839, and All Saints' in Easton, built 1917.

Until the significance of the hidden circle became apparent, it was hard to understand why the architect Thomas Gilbert chose a site that was not only in the middle of an ancient track, but also in a very exposed part of the island. Some say the area was chosen because the soil here is deep enough to dig the required 6 ft for graves. Only 6 years after completion, the graveyard became flooded, necessitating the digging of a large drainage ditch around the churchyard. A short time later in 1795, a storm badly damaged the roof.

## Our Lady and St Andrew's Church, the Grove

The Roman Catholic Church of Our Lady and St Andrew at the Grove is the last church on the circle. Built in 1868, it is set within a row of terraced houses and originally served the growing number of Catholics, which included prison workers, soldiers, sailors and construction gangs working on the breakwater. The architect was Joseph Hansom who designed not only the Hansom Cab

*Our Lady and St Andrew's Church.*

but also the Roman Catholic Cathedral in Plymouth.

According to information received from the Church and the Dorchester Records Office, there is no evidence of a previous ancient building on the site. However, behind the Presbytery there once stood a small stone building said to be the first Roman Catholic Church on the island, existing until 1963. At the back of the present church, you will find a remnant of this building in the form of a holy water font set into the wall of the old mission hall. Also, the gable behind the altar has no window, but strangely the outside wall shows a brick outline of a Gothic arch.

## Ancient Technology

As I pondered over my diagram, I wondered how the surveyors of these churches on the circle built them exactly equidistant from the mother church at Church Ope Cove, bearing in mind its situation – halfway down the cliffs and invisible to the other sites. Researchers have referred to such technology existing in prehistoric times when the megalithic engineers were capable of complex mathematic calculations equal to that of the ancient Egyptians and the Greeks, building their monuments such as Stonehenge and Avebury to precise measurements. Archaeologists named the builders of these unique stone and earth structures the 'Wessex Culture' whose territory included Portland.

St Andrew's Church at Church Ope Cove has been a site of reverence from at least Saxon times and most probably earlier, if the local traditions are true. The fact that the Avalanche Church stands on a knoll and that Southwell has a long-standing tradition of being a substantial Romano-British settlement indicates that the site may be prehistoric. However, there is no current evidence of a previous building beneath St George's, although an ancient stone-lined well, discovered a little south of the church, may indicate an early settlement close by.

During the writing of this book, the discovery of a Romano-British village and medieval buildings beneath the playing fields in Weston, south of St George's Church, brought much excitement to Portland. I discovered that the St Andrew's circle passes through the playing fields to the west of the excavations and probably through an unexcavated part of the same settlement.

# The Circle of St George

Equipped with the knowledge that the church of St George replaced the old sacred centre of St Andrew's, I began to wonder if they replicated another circle, with St George's Church at the centre. So I reversed the process adopted previously, placing the compass point on St George's and the pencil on St Andrew's ruin. To my amazement, this second circle included the impressive church of St Peter's at the Grove, the famous Brackenbury Memorial Church in Fortuneswell, Rufus Castle in Wakeham, and the site of an ancient barrow (burial mound) in Chesil near Brandy Row.

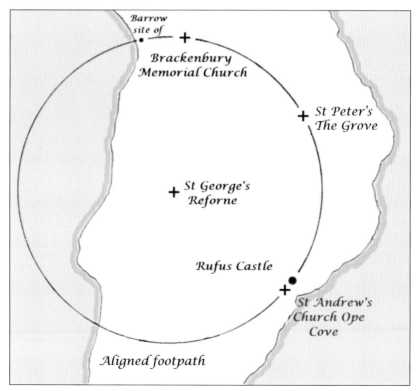

*The circle of St George.*

## St Peter's Church, the Grove

The church of St Peter at the Grove, built of the finest local stone, is a magnificent example of the Romanesque Byzantine style of churches common in the twelfth century. It has a similar layout to early Christian churches, with the altar in the middle of the chancel where the clergy, seated around the semicircular apse, were presided over by the Bishop.

Many guidebooks state that skilled convicts built the church in 1872, although there is a lack of evidence to support this.[6] Originally the church was for the use of military officials in the prison establishments and could seat 550. Curiously, despite the use of cheap labour, the cost of construction at £8000 outweighed that of any other church ever erected on the island.

The arc of the circle passes through the eastern apse of St Peter's where the high altar stands. Sadly, because the building is no longer a place of worship and is now in private hands, I could not enter at this time to inspect the interior, so the following information comes from an old guidebook of St Peter's Church in the local museum archives.

Inside, a polished cross beneath the stained-glass windows casts a shadow of the crucified Jesus over the altar when the light catches it at the right angle. There are fine carved pews, and an open timbered roof made in the old

*St Peter's Church.*

way of using wooden pegs without nails. The beautiful mosaic flooring in the sanctuary and the porch represents the four Evangelists and, according to Peter E.G. Harvey, they are a copy of those in the Palace of the Caesars at Rome.[7] Many years ago, the church became redundant and neglected, until recently; the new owner has great plans to bring it back into the community.

Archaeologist Susann Palmer mentions evidence of an earlier building on or next to this site, referring to excavations in the grounds of the Old Vicarage next door to St Peter's Church, which uncovered two walls:

> *"The earlier one had been robbed or demolished and only the base remained. The later one (which may have contained stones robbed from the earlier) still stood more than a metre high and was very well built. No dateable*

*objects were associated. They are possibly the remains of early ecclesiastical buildings, although there is a possibility that the earlier robbed wall could have been pre-medieval.*[8]

Palmer believes a circular enclosure or estate also existed around the Old Vicarage and St Peter's Church, and that the walled road behind marks part of its outline. Until further excavations take place here, we can only assume that the enclosure was either a small settlement, a farmstead or a ceremonial site such as a henge.

Lord Burleigh's 1539 Tudor map of Portland, now in the Cotton Collection in the British Library, and also included in *Portland, An Illustrated History* by Stuart Morris[9], depicts two beacons behind the Verne. One of them in the Grove area resembles a church tower. Did the Victorian builders of St Peter's have knowledge of this earlier church? When the Tudor antiquarian John Leyland visited Church Ope Cove around 1535, he wrote in his account of the island:

*"Some say that in times past there was another parish church in the Isle but I there learned no certainty of it."*[10]

Fido Lunettes also wrote on his visit to the island:

*"A report prevails arousing the natives that there had been originally three churches upon the island; but it is supported by an authentic testimony."*[11]

According to Elizabeth Pearce, one of these ancient churches existed north of St Andrew's above the Grove where a Monastic Order of the Blackfriars worshipped. Could this be the remnants of the medieval building found close to St Peter's Church? Although I could find no record of the Blackfriars church, there once existed a pier named Blackfriars near King's Pier, north of the Grove, in an area now part of the commercial port.

As you leave the town of Fortuneswell, the road climbs west towards the high plateau where a sharp bend has the curious name of Priory Corner. A local tradition maintains that a religious building built by the Benedictine monks of Winchester existed in this area close to Tout Quarry. This site was a good vantage point for observing anyone approaching the island from the mainland along Chesil Beach, which provided an ideal strategic spot for the monks to build a priory or chapel. The name Tout is an Old English word for 'peep out' or 'look out'. Could this be the third ancient church alluded to by Lunettes that existed along with St Andrew's and possibly Blackfriars at the Grove? It is conceivable that this sacred place also became lost in memory due to the deaths of the monks during the great plague. Unfortunately, the many cliff falls in this area, recalled by locals, may have removed all trace of the building.

## Brackenbury Memorial Church

The next church on the St George circle is the Brackenbury Memorial Church at Fortuneswell, constructed around 1900. The impressive Gothic pinnacle frontage we see today is the result of a competition for the design of a new front façade. The building replaced an earlier perfectly proportioned Wesleyan Chapel originally erected close to the road in 1792 at the expense of Robert Carr Brackenbury, whose friend and mentor was the founding father of Methodism, Charles Wesley. When Brackenbury first arrived in Weymouth in the latter part of the eighteenth century, he asked for directions to Portland, whereupon a local informed him, "It is all Darkness".[10] This was a strange remark considering there was little crime on the island at the time except for the occasional wrecking and looting of ships. Perhaps he was referring to the peculiar marriage and sexual customs unique to Portland. Marriage could not take place until a couple could prove through conception that they were both fertile, certainly not a practice acceptable to a Methodist preacher.

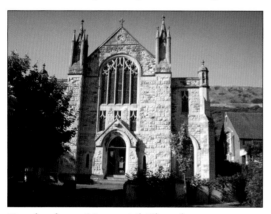

*Brackenbury Memorial Church.*

Brackenbury soon attracted a large following after he preached in a house in Fortuneswell. Later he purchased an area of land in Underhill, below Verne Hill, to build the first Georgian chapel on the island. During the latter part of the nineteenth century, the Underhill congregation became too large for the chapel, and so they planned a larger church. The old chapel was demolished and the new church was built in a different position, much further back off the street, and next door to the previous church. Whoever made the decision to build the church at the new location must have had knowledge of the circle geometry as the later church now falls onto the circumference of the St George circle. Could it have been the powerful Court Leet or the Victorian architects, or was it just a coincidence that they happened to choose a spot whereby the new altar is positioned exactly on the path of the circle? There is certainly no evidence of any prehistoric structures or temples on this site, apart from a rough carved stone water stoop found nearby.

# The Vesica Piscis

The two circles of equal radius centred on the churches of St George and St Andrew overlap to create the mystical symbol of the Vesica Piscis. In Latin, this name literally means the bladder of the fish because of its similar shape when inflated.

The origins of the Vesica symbol are mysterious. Many believe the ancient Pythagoreans first discovered the properties of this unique shape and made it an important part of their teachings. In esoteric lore, the overlapping circles are the merging of different polarities, such as male and female or spirit and matter. In sacred geometry, its symbolism is characterised by the right circle, the realm of spirit, penetrating the left circle, representing the material world. John Michell describes the Vesica Piscis as representing a state of perfect equilibrium between two equal forces.[2]

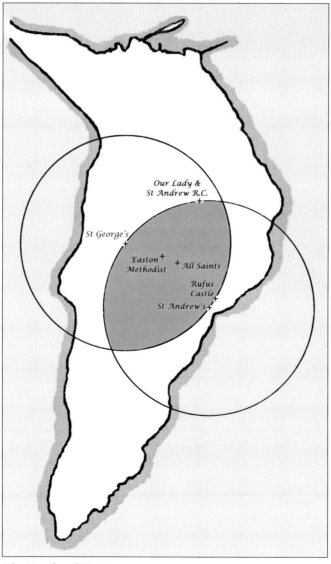

*The Portland Vesica.*

The Vesica has special significance for religious mystics as reflected in the outline of the fish, suggestive of Jesus and the Piscean age, or the womb of the Virgin Mary. The cabalistic Tree of Life identifies the Vesica Piscis as symbolic recognition of the power of the goddess. Medieval architects and stonemasons attached to the Guilds incorporated the Vesica Piscis into the structural design of the Gothic churches and cathedrals around Europe. The knowledge of how to use the Vesica to fix the overall length and breadth of a sacred building was a secret handed down through the mystery schools for over a thousand years.

So, was the Vesica Piscis, as laid down in the sacred geometry of Portland, a symbol of enchantment representing the feminine? Were the designers operative masons belonging to an order who worked with stone locally, or speculative masons who exercised a spiritual programme of self-improvement through a code of beliefs and practices taught by their local Lodge?

The suppression of the feminine, or should I say the 'divine feminine', by the early Roman church in favour of a male-dominated religion has become a hot topic. Yet the medieval stonemasons and architects continued right up until Victorian times to represent feminine symbolism within the design of their churches, based on ancient customs handed down from generation to generation. This knowledge of the 'divine feminine', also held by such secret societies as the Rosicrucians and the Knights Templars, has remained underground from medieval times when such heretical beliefs carried the death sentence.

## Easton Methodist and All Saints' Churches

Perhaps there is a clue to these mysteries inside the churches within the Portland Vesica. Easton, the central village in Portland, has two churches – Easton Methodist and All Saints' Churches. Between the two is the Edwardian Municipal Gardens enclosed within a public square, once the site of Easton Pond. Overlooking the gardens is a grand Methodist church built in 1906 and funded by the people of Portland who raised the entire £7,000 needed for its construction.

On my first visit to the Methodist church, the spacious interior and the beautiful stained-glass windows surprised me. However, the most impressive feature that caught my eye was a fine carving below the pulpit depicting Leonardo da Vinci's famous mural of 'The Last Supper'. In 1914, a journeyman craftsman called Sheppard, a highly skilled stonemason, carved the pulpit on site from a single block of Portland stone with such astonishing detail that I consider it a real treasure and one of the wonders of Portland. He also carved 'The Ascension' over the front porch.

According to many authors, da Vinci incorporated fascinating secrets within many of his paintings in coded symbolism, particularly in 'The Last Supper'. Here a figure seated next to Christ appears to be a woman, believed by many researchers to be Mary Magdalene, an idea made famous by the book *The Da Vinci Code*. I found it fascinating that within Portland's landscape Vesica, the

*'The Last Supper' at Easton Methodist Church. (With kind permission of Easton Methodist Church.)*

womb of the goddess, I find the perfect representation of the divine feminine in da Vinci's depiction.

On the other side of the gardens, behind the shops, is All Saints' Church, referred to by Portlanders as 'the grandest church in the isle'. Within a tree-

*All Saints' Church, Easton.*

lined field, the architect George Crickmay designed and built a new parish church in 1917 in classic Gothic style to replace St George's at Reforne. The original plan included a tower, but for some reason this never left the drawing board. The interior boasts a magnificent east window, a memorial to the soldiers of the First World War. It depicts Christ within what appears to be a Vesica symbol guarded by St George and St Michael; I have often found that the old stonemasons, architects and artisans of the stained-glass windows portrayed ancient knowledge as allegory.

On the ceiling above the altar is another of the wonders of Portland, twelve beautifully painted panels depicting various animals and angels referred to as the 'Beasts of the Apocalypse'. Upon closer observation, I noticed that they are in fact symbols representing the twelve signs of the zodiac. The church guide refers to a Portland tale that Mr Barnes Griggs, the builder of All Saints' and Rector of Portland from 1909 to 1931, invited a party of students from Oxford to paint the roof with pictures and emblems of the Saints. He was later appalled to find they had painted the signs of the zodiac instead.

*The painted ceiling showing the twelve astrological signs in All Saints' Church. (With kind permission of All Saints' Church.)*

The zodiac above the altar is certainly an unusual sight, as it bears no relation to traditional church beliefs. On the other hand, astrology and sacred geometry are part of the pre-Christian imagery often incorporated into churches by stonemasons and Freemasons. Painted signs of the zodiac can be found on the ceilings of many Masonic Lodges throughout the world and represent the progress of the sun through each sign or the 12 steps of the Freemason, with each sign having its own mystical interpretation.

The reredos or screen behind the altar displays four shields depicting the emblems of island saints, seemingly representing the five key churches on the two circles. On the right are the Keys of St Peter (at the Grove), next is the cross of St Andrew (at Church Ope Cove and Southwell), followed by the cross of St George (in Reforne), and finally Our Lady and the infant Jesus (Catholic Church of Our Lady and St Andrew, at the Grove).

Although the guidebook states that these shields represent the four island saints, there appears to be one missing – St John the Baptist. This is curious because St John the Baptist's Church in Fortuneswell was built long before All Saints' Church. Maybe its absence is a result of the cultural differences between the people of Underhill and Tophill. Alternatively, this church may have its own unique mystery, which I reveal later in the book.

# The Old Solar Festivals

King Warry wrote that All Saints' Church stands upon a sacred 'Mark Point'. The old straight track between the ancient harbour at the Mere and St Andrew's at Church Ope Cove deviates around the area of All Saints for some reason, as if it may "… bring some dire calamity in its train". She also added that on this mark point:

> "… may have been a Barrow used as a sighting point to help determine the position of maybe the rising sun or of some particular star, an all powerful factor in Neolithic and even latter days."[12]

On a map of Portland, King Warry found an alignment of sites, or a ley line, that intersects with this ancient road at the 'Mark Point'. Starting from the east coast, the line begins at a stone circle, seen by King Warry in the late Victorian period standing at the edge of the cliffs at the end of Grove Road, and then through another destroyed by convicts to make a grotto in the Prison Governor's garden. The line continues through All Saints' Church and the recent archaeological excavations at Weston to Blacknor Fort, once the site of a beacon on the west cliffs and possibly an Iron Age enclosure. I realised that this ley is oriented towards the Beltane sunrise, an important prehistoric and Celtic solar festival. Considering that King Warry wrote *The High Place* around 1908, her concept of astro-archaeology and ley lines was way ahead of its time.

Turning my attention to alignments, I noticed that the orientation of the axis of the Vesica Piscis, which is a line drawn between St George's and St Andrew's at Church Ope Cove, is 133 degrees east of north. This bearing at this latitude is the direction of sunrise on the winter solstice. Many ancient pagan cultures around the world regard the winter solstice as an extremely important and sacred event, when the sun symbolically dies and is reborn into a new year. A great number of prehistoric monuments around the British Isles and Europe are oriented to this direction to observe the sunrise on this particular day. In the opposite direction, this solar line from St George's is oriented towards the north-west, which observes sunset at the summer solstice. The ancient cultures of the Middle East believed this maximum setting of the sun signified the route that souls travelled on their journey to the ancestral planes.

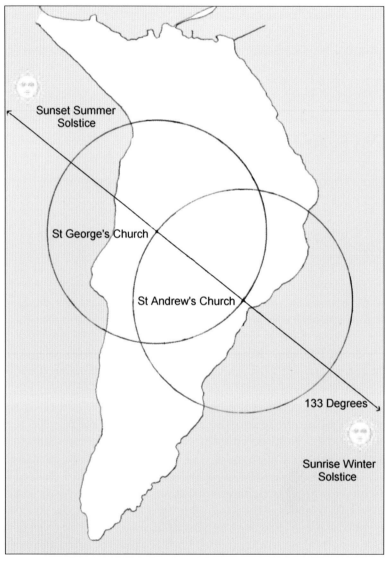

*Solar alignment of St George's and St Andrew's Churches.*

Earlier, I mentioned that the new site proposed for St George's Church appeared unsuitable because of its exposure to the elements and its location in the middle of an ancient track. Robert Pearce also adds:

*"It would not be becoming on my part to question the wisdom of the gentlemen in selecting the site for the new church at Reforne. At that time it had to serve for the needs of the whole island. It seems, however, today too much removed from the centres of population. This has perhaps been a source of weakness to it, especially with the many other places of worship erected in the very midst of the people."[13]*

I believe that Thomas Gilbert deliberately chose this new site to align with St Andrew's on a winter solstice axis, as if to continue the ancient practice of sun worship.

The Court Leet dedicated the new church to 'St George of England', King George II having given £500 towards the cost of building it. The real reason might be the symbolic relationship between St George and St Andrew and the old pagan festivals (see Chapter 7).

*The Heavenly Twins in the east window at All Saints' Church. (With kind permission of All Saints' Church.)*

Another relative point of interest is that, in sacred geometry, the circle on the left in the Vesica Piscis represents the material world while the right circle symbolises the world of spirit. Likewise, St George is the earthly material counterpart of St Michael in their roles as the Heavenly Twins. According to Alan Insole, "The cult of the Heavenly Twins, or Sons of Thunder, was at one time widely distributed over the whole world".[14] The Heavenly Twins are the benevolent friends of man, the Good Saviours to whom we appeal in times of strife and war. Accompanying the twins is the storm god Indra (Andrew),[15] who, according to some cultures, is also known as the sky god, representing the realm of spirit. The Twins appear as St George and St Michael in the east window of All Saints' Church beneath the zodiac ceiling representing the heavens.

The worship of St Andrew may have its roots in pre-Christian festivals held on a sacred day that later became a Christianised Saint's Day. St Andrew's Day (30 November) is not a known pagan day but a Christian time of Advent. Advent is the beginning of the Church Year for most churches in the Western tradition, a time to prepare for the Lord, the King that is to come. It begins on the fourth Sunday before Christmas Day, which is the Sunday nearest to St Andrew's Day.

In 1752, protestant England finally succumbed to the earlier Catholic Gregorian calendar to solve the problem of additional years accumulating in our own Julian calendar. The Gregorian calendar dropped 11 days from the Julian calendar to rectify this. Before the changes, the festival of St Andrew used to fall on 11 December, only 11 days before the winter solstice. If you add 11 days to the present St George's Day, 23 April, we get within a day of when the old Portlanders used to celebrate their May Day festivals.

It seems obvious to me that in the old religion the festival of St Andrew, which now celebrates the coming of the Lord, was actually a time to prepare for the death of the sun god – before the sun symbolically dies as it reaches its most southerly sunrise – called the winter solstice. In other parts of Britain, St Andrew's Day was the traditional day to slaughter the cattle. So, symbolically, St George heralds the light of new growth and St Andrew heralds the days of sacrifice and darkness.

Pagan festivals once took place on a site opposite the Brackenbury Memorial Church and a clue to this lies in the earlier place name of that area, Paradise. Paradise is an old name found all over England at sites where ancient spring festivals took place, such as Paradise Hill near Glastonbury Tor and Old Paradise in London.[14] Indeed pagan veneration continued on Portland right up to the nineteenth century. There is a building in Chesil with an external staircase leading to an upper room called the Conjuror's Lodge, so-named because between 1816 and 1826 this room became a place of worship for a breakaway group of island Methodists accused of practising witchcraft. Robert Pearce comments:

*"Superstition and the belief in witchcraft had so possessed the minds of the people, and among them several of the most prominent members of the Methodists, that indeed very serious injury was being done through this belief. Almost every event was supposed to be regulated by this evil power, and every misfortune was attributed to the witch."[13]*

# Chapter 5

# Stonemasons and Secret Knowledge

During my research of the Vesica, I found an intriguing link between Saint Andrew and the early stonemasons, whilst on holiday in Amalfi, Italy. Amalfi is an ancient port southeast of Naples and a base for tourists to explore the famous spectacular coastline. I was particularly intrigued by the cathedral as it houses the shrine and relics of St Andrew the Apostle in the crypt.

Between AD 839 and 1135, Amalfi was regarded as the premier Maritime Republic in Italy and a cosmopolitan centre of trade for the whole of the Mediterranean. Amalfi laws allowed no religious prejudices and encouraged

*The tower of the old cathedral, Amalfi.*

trade with the Saracens, an act that eventually resulted in Amalfi being excommunicated by Pope John VIII. Travelling as far as Antioch, Byzantium and Alexandria, the visiting merchants enriched the port with precious fabrics, perfumes and spices from the Orient. It seemed that Amalfi was an open door to the west for Islamic and Arabic stonemasons, who first introduced the use of the Vesica shape into architecture.[1] However, because the town suffered complete destruction in AD 1013 and 1343 by massive tidal waves, I had difficulty in finding any evidence of this within the architecture of the town.

Nevertheless, the medieval stonemasons of Amalfi did use the Vesica within the design of the frontage of the cathedral and its cloisters during their renovation. Interestingly, the bell tower stands separate to the main building and is architecturally different from the cathedral, being Islamic in design. Just below the roof of the tower, I could see the Vesica design interlaced around the structure. Looking through the guidebook, I discovered that the tower is the only surviving part of the old cathedral built in 1180. On closer inspection, I also noticed ancient masonry at the base of this tower that may date from the time when the Arab masons first settled in Amalfi.

As I explored the narrow streets, I discovered a beautifully carved seven-chain Vesica Piscis relief set into a section of wall, obviously the remains from a very early building perhaps destroyed by one of the tidal waves. I also discovered

*Remnants of an old building in Amalfi.*

that the Military Hospitaller Order of St John of Jerusalem originated in Amalfi and used the town as a major port from AD 1050–1291. In the old portion of the cathedral is a wall painting of their first Grand Master, Gerardo Sasso, born within the territory of Amalfi. During his reign, Pope Pascal awarded the Order a Papal Bull, granting exemption from church control. They even adopted the ancient white eight-pointed cross of Amalfi as their emblem, which still survives today in the symbol of the Order of St John. I believe that this ancient order including the Knights Templars protected not just the pilgrims but also the stonemasons whose treasure was the knowledge of sacred geometry. Perhaps it is no coincidence that in Amalfi Cathedral we have the first use of the Vesica in western architecture *and* the bones of St Andrew.

The shrine in the crypt has a statue of the saint holding two golden fish, also repeated in a mosaic above the main door of the cathedral. Does this refer to the story that Andrew was a fisherman or is it allegorical, as a fish also represents the Vesica Piscis? Were the Amalfi masons leaving us a clue that St Andrew is associated with sacred geometry? If this is the case, the dedication of three churches to St Andrew on Portland must also be a clue to the hidden Vesica Piscis.

*St Andrew and the fishes at Amalfi Cathedral.*

The first church built on Portland after St George's to substantiate the circle of St Andrew is the Catholic Church of Our Lady and St Andrew at the Grove, built in 1868. Unusually it has no east window; instead, it has a great Gothic arch, or the top half of a Vesica, outlined in the exterior of the wall. The mystery of this arch now becomes clear when you realise that this little church lies near the intersection of the two arcs or arch of the Portland Vesica. The second and most important church to define the Vesica is St Peter's, built just down the road from Our Lady in 1872. I also had a sense that this church may contain further clues to the Vesica and the mystery of the Portland geometry.

# Inside St Peter's Church

*The mosaic floor.*

Although no longer open to the public, I was given an opportunity to view the interior of St Peter's Church. The first feature that drew my attention was the western rose window with eight petals, each one containing the Seal of Solomon, a six-pointed star made from two interlocking equilateral triangles held within a circle. Within each of the Seals is an angel playing a musical instrument. The inner circle of the window has eight segments around a central circle radiating an eight-pointed star, which connects with each Seal of Solomon. The mosaic floor of the semicircular apse by the altar also displays six-pointed stars along with triangles and circles.

The eight petals of the rose window could be interpreting the eight seasonal rituals observed in the Celtic year. These are:

- Samhain or Halloween (31 October);
- Yule or the winter solstice (21 December);
- Imbolc (around 1 February);
- Oestre, celebrating the beginning of spring at the vernal equinox (21 March);
- Beltane, the beginning of summer (1 May);
- Litha or Midsummer's Day (24 June);
- Lammas or Lughnasadh (1 August);
- Mabon, the autumn equinox and beginning of harvest (21 September).

This eight-pointed symbol appears in many different traditions the world over; in some cultures it is a sun wheel said to be symbolic of the goddess Ishtar. At the Vatican in Rome, the Christian centre of power, this symbol also appears

*The rose window in St Peter's.*

in St Peter's Square. In Native American traditions, this star is said to have deep significance, often painted on wall hangings and incorporated into their weavings. Rod Bearcloud of the Star Nation People believes it relates to sacred sound and resonance and can be heard in the sound of a drum and in the tones that we manifest from instruments and our voices. This musical connection reveals itself in the rose window in St Peter's – the eight angel musicians within the eight Seals of Solomon may represent the eight notes of the scale and the law of octaves.

## The Seal of Solomon

In Freemasonic symbolism, the Seal of Solomon has six points with a seventh at its centre. This centre represents God, from which all geometry extends and to which everything else around relates. It also connects with the central phallic figure representing Baal in the sun worship symbol. The two equilateral triangles that make up the Seal of Solomon represent the male and female, or positive and negative – the duality of the three-dimensional world in which we live. Even the name Solomon has significance in relation to the Seal, although some historians see him as fictional and no record of him exists other than in the Bible. His name contains two syllables: Sol, the masculine Sun, and Mon, the feminine Moon. The origin of Solomon's Seal is very obscure and many researchers have found that it dates farther back in time than the Jews and King David to the ancient cultures of India and Egypt. The Seal was also a Phoenician symbol and has its roots in the esoteric practices and occult schools of the ancient mystics including the Druids. The Grove area on Portland once had many ancient stones associated with the Druids.

A Seal of Solomon also links the Portland churches. The Brackenbury Memorial Church in Fortuneswell is significant as it is located upon the Vesica Piscis as well as on the northern apex of the Seal. This chapel replaced an earlier Methodist building nearer the main road and outside of the geometry. This indicates that it was the later Victorian builders who had knowledge of the geometry.

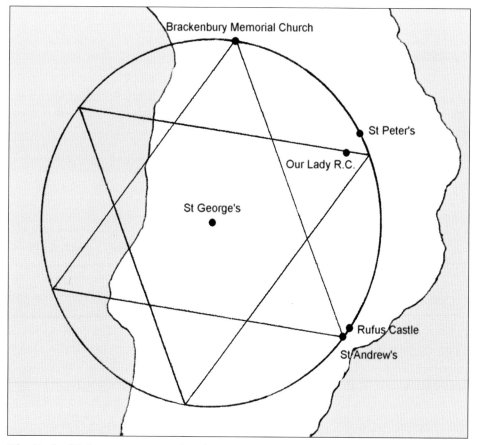

*The Seal of Solomon over Portland.*

Nevertheless, the Seal of Solomon only has significance to the St George circle and not the St Andrew circle. I was yet to discover an important link between the six-pointed star and the Vesica Piscis that would solve the secret of the Masonic code on Portland. Sometime later, after studying sacred geometry from Masonic teachings described in a few published books, I found the key to unlock the riddle of the geometry. In *The Secrets of Solomon's Temple* by K.L. Gest[2], the Vesica Piscis has the capacity to create all forms of sacred geometry including Solomon's Seal.

First, you must define a centre by drawing a vertical line from top to bottom where the two circles of the Vesica intersect and a horizontal line through the centres of the circles. Then by placing a compass point where the lines cross and the pencil at the top intersection, draw a new circle as shown in Fig. 1. Then proceed as shown in Figs 2, 3 and 4.

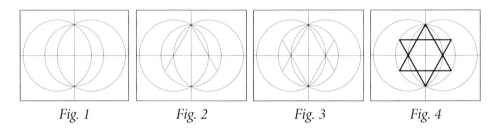

*Fig. 1*          *Fig. 2*          *Fig. 3*          *Fig. 4*

When I placed the Seal of Solomon over the plan of the Portland Vesica no other churches or significant sites fitted with the plan until further research on the history of the Portland Freemasons provided another clue.

## The Freemasons

I was amazed to find that for such a small island there are six Masonic Lodges. Portland Lodge is the oldest; others include the Loyal Manor Lodge, Vindelis Lodge, Quintus Lodge, Chesil Lodge and the United Service Lodge.

In 1864, members of the All Souls' Lodge in Weymouth decided to investigate the possibility of opening a Lodge on Portland for the military forces and other new members wanting to join the Craft. Meetings began at the Royal Breakwater Hotel, moving after 15 years to a new building called Portland Hall at the Gas Works in Victoria Square. Subsequently, the success of the Lodge called for an even larger building, now the present Masonic Hall opposite. A grand gathering of influential Masons assembled on Portland for the laying of the foundation stone on 23 June 1898. This day is significant, for it is the eve of St John the Baptist's day, which heralds the New Year for Freemasons and Knights Templars. This date also commemorates the laying of the foundation cornerstone of St Paul's Cathedral in 1675, witnessed by the greatest gathering of Freemasons ever seen.[3]

The foundations of the first churches on Portland that define the Vesica date to 4 years after Freemasonry began on Portland, a period when the population began to increase dramatically. In fact, between 1851 and 1900 the population tripled from 5,000 to 15,000, necessitating the building of new places of worship around the island.

I began at first to suspect that the knowledge of sacred geometry brought with the Freemasons to Portland inspired the locals to create the Vesica Piscis. Yet, it is unlikely that this new fraternity would have had much influence over the long-established Court Leet whose decisions included church building, unless of course members of the Court Leet were part of an already existing secret Lodge on the island, or members of the new lodge. Elizabeth Pearce recalled a number of stonemasons settling on the island after the building of St Paul's Cathedral in London.[4] Did these foreigners, ancestors of the stonemasons who built London, belong to a secret fraternity on Portland?

Although many authors consider that the people responsible for landscape geometry were megalithic engineers, ancient Greeks or the medieval Knights Templars, I believe the Freemasons were responsible for the Portland geometry. Although the history of Freemasonry officially began with the opening of the Grand Lodge of England in 1777, its true origins are controversial. Freemasonic historians generally accept that there is an historical connection with the stonemasons or operative masons and the builders of the great medieval castles and cathedrals in Europe. Many of the ceremonies and rituals in today's lodges are veiled in allegory, a term meaning a narrative describing a subject under the guise of another, a technique that allows only those initiated to understand their true meaning. Most modern researchers into Freemasonic secrets believe that they have a basis in geometry, alchemy and astrology, a knowledge handed down to them by the ancient stonemasons.

Laurence Gardner states "… the representation of a point within a circle is the most significant of all symbols in freemasonry".[5] My research into Masonic knowledge revealed that the next progression of the point within a circle is the Vesica Piscis from which every form of geometry, including Solomon's Seal and the pentagram, is born.

Gardner also quotes the *Regius Manuscript* dated 1390, the oldest Masonic document in Britain, now in the British Museum, which records an account of King Athelstan of Mercia (AD 930) and the rules of conduct laid down for his council of stonemasons and apprentices. According to Baigent and Leigh, Masonic legend tells of Freemasonry in England beginning with King Athelstan, who became an architect and master builder:

> *"Athelstan's son is said to have joined an already existing fraternity of Masons, became an enthusiastic member himself and, by dint of his status, obtained a 'free charter' for his brethren. As a result of this royal recognition,*

> *a Masonic conclave is supposed to have been convened at York and the regulations drafted which formed the basis of English Freemasonry.*"[6]

During the reign of Athelstan (AD 924–940), a most ambitious building project began – that of York Minster. For the first time in England, new techniques incorporated influences from Islamic and Judaic cultures. The spread of Islam into Spain in the seventh and eighth centuries brought a style of building into Europe using the Vesica Piscis. This knowledge of sacred geometry continued northwards into England with the French stonemasons to the Saxon court of King Athelstan.

Athelstan, the grandson of Alfred the Great, may have utilised this new fraternity of stonemasons to build Milton Abbey in Dorset, then the centre of his kingdom of Wessex. I also discovered that he built many stone churches around Dorset and founded settlements on the mainland opposite Portland. King Warry hinted at a connection between Athelstan and the Saxon church at Church Ope Cove on Portland when she stated:

> *"Athelstan finally defeated the last Prince of Cornwall, Howel, in 936. A mound at the bottom of Higher Lane called Mound Owl – a corruption of Howel – traditionally covered the remains of two Saxon princes, killed in a great battle. Could this mound have been connected in any way with Athelstan's victories in the West? If so it implies close association with the manor, and the probability of his intimate connection with the erection of a Saxon church [on Portland] whose life was brief." [7]*

It would be remarkable if Athelstan, one of the founding fathers of Freemasonry in England, built St Andrew's Church at Church Ope Cove.

An earlier link with Freemasonry in England is through St Alban, born in the third century in Hertfordshire near Verulamium, present-day St Albans. According to legend, Amphibalus, a Roman Christian, reintroduced the Craft into Britain through St Alban at a time when the practice of Freemasonry was in decline. St Alban's Head, the most southerly point in Purbeck near Worth Matravers, Dorset, was a significant sighting point for the Druids standing at the Grove on Portland. Alban is a name considered to be a corruption of St Aldhelm who died in AD 709, as the ancient chapel of St Aldhelm still stands on the headland dedicated to him. However, if we consider the close links between stonemasons and Freemasons it is more likely that the operative stonemasons, i.e. those working in stone in the neighbouring Purbeck quarries, named the headland after their founding father St Alban.

Although Freemasonry continued to flourish during the Victorian period, many of the ancient secrets of the order had been lost during the reign of King Charles II and the revolution of 1688. Because of this, the United Grand Lodge of England, established in 1813, began with little of the true knowledge of the origins and traditions of the earlier Freemasons. The Rev James Anderson, quoted by Gardner (2005), blamed Christopher Wren for the lack of available Masonic literature:

> *"Anderson was convinced that Wren, a founder member of the Royal Society, was fully aware of secrets that the Hanoverian fraternity wanted to know – but he died without revealing anything."*[5]

Consequently, it is possible that the Victorian Freemasons had little idea of the true secrets of sacred geometry. I later found that the Portlanders, in their isolation, may have kept Wren's legacy alive.

# Sir Christopher Wren

At this point in my investigations, I suspected that Wren was integral to the unfolding geometry on Portland, and that his life and work needed further scrutiny.

Born in 1632 at East Knoyle in Wiltshire, Wren grew up during the second Renaissance that heralded a new resurgence in philosophy and science. He showed great intellectual ability in many fields including astronomy and medicine; his inventive genius likened him to Leonardo da Vinci. He became a member of All Souls, an elite group of philosophers whose members included Robert Boyle, John Evelyn and John Wilkins.

His association with members of All Souls later helped to found the so-called Invisible College of philosophers inspired by the teachings of Francis Bacon, known also as The Royal Society. The term Invisible College refers to an elite 'Brotherhood' or secret society whose goal was to encourage the betterment of humanity through the expansion of knowledge and performing good deeds. Many of its members were Rosicrucians and Freemasons and it is almost certain that Wren became a member of the Craft. During the restoration of the monarchy, Charles II awarded the College a more official foundation.

During this period of religious freedom and enlightenment, Wren chose to explore the mysteries of the Earth and the cosmos. He discovered how the ancient mysteries could merge with architecture using sacred geometry.

In 1665, he received his greatest commission, the redesign of the tower of old St Paul's Cathedral. To gain inspiration for this, he embarked on an architectural tour of France where he met the great Italian designer Bernini. He arrived back in England in March 1666 and submitted his plans for a new dome, accepted on 27 August, a week before the Great Fire. After the disaster, Wren submitted further plans to King Charles II to rebuild London, inspired by the architecture and monumental avenues of Paris. His idea was to replace the winding and congested old streets of London with a mystical design to include an octagonal plaza near the site of London's Templar headquarters. Avenues leading from here and plazas around London were to be based on the Hebrew Cabala and 'heavenly bodies'.[8] Wren probably passed this knowledge of astronomy and architecture on to his son, also named Christopher, who later described London as "a city particularly favoured by the celestial influences, a Pandora, on which each planet has contributed something".[9]

With the ending of papal authority in England, architects could now establish a new centre of religious power in the capital, not unlike the Vatican. The site chosen was St Paul's Cathedral, a sacred hill where a temple of Diana once stood. The architect elected to build it was Sir Christopher Wren, and the stone chosen was Portland Whitbed.

During the quarrying and transportation of Portland stone used for St Paul's, Wren frequently visited the island, most probably staying at the home of architect Thomas Gilbert. Wren continued to be surveyor of the quarries until 1717, having close links with Portland until his death in 1723; he even represented Weymouth as MP in 1702.

## The Master Architect

The Gilbert family were certainly true Portlanders, having lived on the island from at least the thirteenth century. The father and grandfather of Thomas Gilbert, the architect of St George's Church, were both called Thomas and worked alongside Christopher Wren while in charge of the Portland stone trade. Grandfather Gilbert's appointment by Wren as agent to the quarries came after serious mismanagement by the former agent Thomas Knight. In 1695, Thomas the father continued to work closely with Wren until completion of the project.

The Gilbert family home in Fortuneswell, built around 1710, is a splendid example of Queen Anne domestic architecture and was probably built by Thomas the father. Eric Ricketts mentions that the house included architectural elements that could be right out of Wren's drawing office.[10]

If we return to the period just before the building of St George's Church, when the situation of old St Andrew's was very precarious, a parish vestry meeting was held to consider whether to build a new church or repair the existing one. This key meeting, held on 30 August 1753, involved the most important people on the island, including master architect Thomas Gilbert.

On 22 November of that year, a report given to the committee revealed that the cost of renovating and making safe the church of St Andrew far outweighed the cost of building a new church on a different site. Plans were submitted for the building of St George's in a more convenient part of the island. Thomas Gilbert chose a piece of ground in a place called Wide Street at the western end of Reforne to build a "well-defined church capable of receiving at least six hundred persons". King George II gave £500 towards the cost of building, the rest being met by local landowners John and Richard Tucker, and Knights of the Shire George Pitt and Humphrey Sturt.[11]

Ricketts also mentions that there is little evidence of any work by Gilbert before or after he produced magnificent plans for St George's Church. *The Royal Commission on Historical Monuments, Volume 2,*[12] suggests that the design of St George's Church reflects the work of the artificer (designer or craftsman) rather than of the architect. As a child, Thomas Gilbert would have known Wren on Wren's visits to his father and grandfather, and Wren may well have later influenced Gilbert's design for St George's Church. On the other hand, knowing that St Andrew's Church had an uncertain future, it is possible that Wren drew up plans for St George's during his earlier visits.

I believe the Gilberts had links with early Freemasonry, because there is a mention of Thomas Gilbert of Portland (grandfather) being a member of The London Masons Company,[11] a very old establishment granted Arms in 1473.[13] Their coat of arms, which includes three castles and compasses, amalgamated with the later arms of the Metropolitan Grand Lodge of London in 2003. It is almost certain that his son and grandson, the architect of St George's, would also have been members, initiated into the Craft in the time-honoured way from father to son.

If the early teachings of Freemasonry, which included sacred geometry, died with Wren as Gardner states, then it is possible that the Gilberts kept Wren's legacy alive. Edward Condor, a former Grand Master of The London Masons Company of which the Gilberts were members, wrote of the significance of the Vesica Piscis in *The Hole Craft and Fellowship of Masonry.*[14]

# The Symmetry of St George's Church

Because the Vesica Piscis is the seed from which all geometry is born, I was not surprised to discover that many pre-Reformation architects designed their churches using a measure based on this figure, or indeed multiples of this figure such as the chained Vesica. I then wondered if the architect Gilbert, or possibly even Wren, continued this ancient practice in the design of St George's Church. With an accurate ground plan of the church obtained from the Redundant Churches Fund, I began to explore the geometry with pen, compass and ruler.

The crossing of the two lines that define the main axis and the transepts of the church proved to be at the exact centre of its length, directly under the dome. Therefore, a circle drawn from this sacred centre creates the equal-armed cross within a circle, as shown in the figure overleaf.

Using a compass placed at the intersections of the line and circle, I further discovered that the whole church, and some of its internal features, fits accurately within a double Vesica within a double Vesica within a double

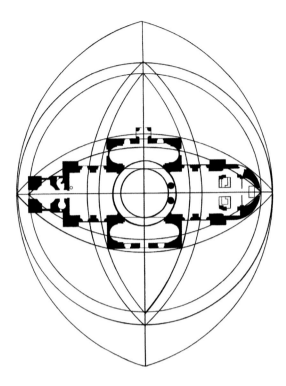

*Plan of St George's Church showing perfect Vesica Piscis geometry. (The drawing was carried out by Lewis Brown Chartered Land Surveyors 2007, with kind permission from the Churches Conservation Trust. The opinions and analysis offered by the author are his alone.)*

circle. Furthermore, a double circle drawn from the sacred centre to the supporting walls of the dome and the inner borders of its axis determine the positioning of the pulpits.

As you walk from the tower to the altar inside the church, you can see an interesting symbolic progression from base matter to spiritual unity. The four-sided base of the tower is representative of the phallic masculine force, confined within square dimensions. As you move towards the sacred centre of the church, the metal stud set into the floor indicates 'the point within a circle', from which the Vesica geometry evolves. Here, at the centre, we connect with the feminine forces symbolised by the circular dome above, and from here you progress in union towards the spiritual high altar – a marriage of the square and the circle, or matter and spirit.

St George's Church is an exceptional building as it displays the perfect proportions of sacred geometry in a unique arrangement of the Vesica Piscis.

# The All-Seeing Eye

I decided to visit the old Masonic Hall in Victoria Square, now specialist accommodation for divers, to see if there were any further clues to the mystery of the Portland geometry. On the bay window at the front of the building are Freemasonic symbols of sacred geometry including the Seal of Solomon. Below the window are four lion heads that, according to the owner, used to have names. In Masonic lore, they are symbols of protection, sovereignty and strength.

Inside, on the main fireplace, are three Masonic symbols. The middle symbol

*Masonic symbols on the old Masonic Hall.*

is the Masonic 'square and compass', the tools that create sacred geometry. On the right is the 'plumb rule', used to test the uprightness of walls and the 'level' to prepare the base of a column. The left symbol is the Seal of Solomon but with an internal triangle. I researched this symbol and discovered that it embodies all platonic solids and the law of the unity of opposites. On the roof gable above the present false ceiling is a carving of an eye, which during the time the building was a Masonic Hall overlooked members of the Craft.

*Masonic symbols on the fireplace inside the old Masonic Hall.*

Applying the platonic symbol to the Portland Vesica Piscis and adding a central circle within the triangle brings the two most impressive churches of All Saints and the Easton Methodist into the overall geometry. Finally, we have one overall divine plan that connects all the major churches in the shape of an eye.

In the world of the occult, the eye is a symbol of the deity known as the 'All-Seeing Eye' and used as a means of protection. The Freemasons refer to this icon as the Eye of Providence, representing the all-seeing eye of God. It is a reminder for them that God, the Grand Architect of the Universe, observes the deeds of the Mason. William Schnoebelen, in his controversial book *Masonry:*

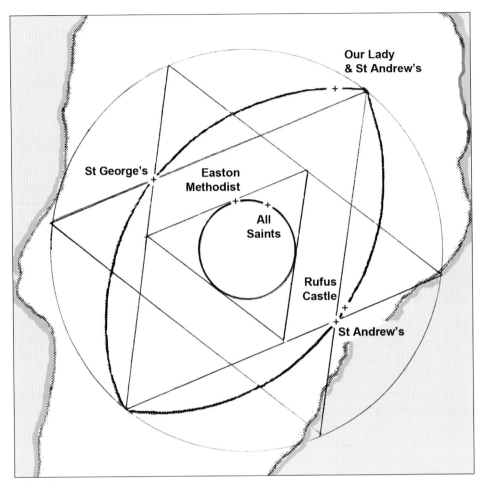

*The All-Seeing Eye.*

*Beyond the Light*, states that the Masonic 'third degree lecture' teaches that the

> *"All-Seeing Eye, whom the Sun, Moon and Stars obey, and under whose watchful care even comets perform their stupendous revolutions, beholds the innermost recesses of the human heart, and will reward us according to our works."*[15]

The Eye of Providence has rays of light extending down from below the eye, or seen within a triangle, as shown on the Great Seal of the United States. This may indicate the role of the Freemasons in the founding of America. There are other variations seen in Masonic temples, with the eye itself being replaced by the letter G, representing not only God but also the art of Geometry.

The eye is also an ancient symbol of the sun, and played an important part in the magical traditions and mystery schools of the Egyptians, who associated the eye with their gods Osiris and Horus.

I believe the Portland Freemasons left clues to the island geometry in the designs of St Peter's Church, St George's Church and in the old Masonic Hall, with the eye on the upper wall and the symbols on the fireplace. There is some controversy, however, over whether prisoners actually constructed St Peter's; if they did, they were undoubtedly under the guidance and management of the architect who was most certainly a Freemason.

Next door to the Easton Methodist Church is the old Wesleyan School built in 1818. Below the Vesica apex of the front Gothic window is a double Vesica with a central circle, mirroring the geometry of St George's Church.

*Wesleyan School window in Easton.*

During my research of the Freemasons, one other fact came to light, namely the close link between the monastic orders and the stonemasons. The early stonemasons lived in seclusion with the monks, protected by the monasteries they built. In fact, there is evidence that these powerful stonemasons practised their ceremonies in their own separate buildings, protected by the walls of the monastery.

Some of the Benedictine monks who settled on Portland may have been stonemasons of that order, whose job was to carve the stone on site. Perhaps their temple may have been the imposing building that once stood opposite the Mermaid Inn built around 1250, later becoming the residence of the vicar of St Andrew's. Leland in 1540 described it as "the best building in the isle"; islanders know this building by various names: the Parsonage, the Vicarage and the Oratory. A nineteenth century drawing shows the ruins looking more like a classic Gothic church than a rectory. Cromwell and his men targeted the building by burning it to the ground, at the same time destroying all the early records of Portland therein. These records may have included accounts and transactions written by the Benedictine and Blackfriar monks, as well as Masonic records. The Vicarage, to use one of its names, remained as a romantic ruin until quarrying finally sealed its fate in 1917.

The Old Vicarage, Wakeham. (Courtesy of Dorset County Museum. Originally published 12 March 1784 by S. Hooper.)

# Chapter 6

# Leys and Alignments

A remarkable ley on Portland connects three churches and a chapel in a north–south alignment. As shown on the map (see left), this line passes through the tower of St John the Baptist's Church in Fortuneswell, the altar of St George's Church, the Primitive Methodist Chapel at Weston, and the western front of St Andrew's Church at Southwell. The odds of this four-point ley being the result of chance are thousands to one.

Many ley lines pass through churches built over prehistoric markers such as standing stones, tumuli or long barrows. Our ancient ancestors may have built them to mark a network or grid formed by the electromagnetic emissions of the Earth, detectable only to animals, psychics and dowsers. However, some of these alignments may have been lines of sight toward the horizon to mark the rising of a particular star, or, as previously discovered, part of a divine geometric plan devised by ancient and modern geomancers to link their holy places.

This particular alignment on Portland may be a meridian. Ancient cultures around the world created a meridian as a longitude line for mapping and measuring distances. This line also marks the path of the sun, when it reaches its zenith at noon on the summer solstice. Our ancestors honoured this event, believing the sun god was then at his most powerful and influential position in the heavens. King Warry refers to the old customs performed by her elders when Midsummer's Day was a celebrated event on Portland, and everyone except those who were disabled or too old made their way to the bonfires at the Bill or Beal.[1]

*Reproduced from the 1903 Ordnance Survey map.*

71

The four main churches have different dates of construction: 1754 for St George's, 1839 for St John's, 1850 for the Methodist Chapel at Weston and 1879 for the Avalanche Church at Southwell. I believe this line corresponds to a Victorian Masonic plan to align the churches along with St George's to this important solar orientation.

Freemasons herald St John the Baptist and the later St John the Evangelist as patron saints of their order, their feast days becoming major Masonic festivals throughout the world. To our ancient ancestors the solstices were important religious days celebrating the birth and death of the sun. The early church adopted these festivals as feast days. The summer solstice was fixed to 24 June and dedicated to St John the Baptist, and the winter solstice was fixed to 27 December and dedicated to St John the Evangelist. England's first Grand Lodge officially opened on 24 June 1717, the feast day of St John the Baptist, and became the United Grand Lodge of England on 27 December 1813, the feast day of St John the Evangelist. Therefore, St John the Baptist's day is a day of beginnings, and the day of the Evangelist is that of endings.

In most Masonic Lodges you will find a symbol showing a point within a circle bordered by two perpendicular parallel lines. These lines represent St John the Baptist and St John the Evangelist. As the Freemason symbolically travels the cycle of a solar year he touches the lines of St John the Baptist (summer solstice) and St John the Evangelist (winter solstice), the circle representing a clock of one solar year, from winter solstice to summer solstice, then back to winter solstice. The Portland meridian line mirrors one of the parallel lines bordering the Masonic 'point within a circle', only the point referred to in this case is St Andrew's Church and the circle is the ring of churches. Furthermore, at the top of the meridian is St John the Baptist's Church in Fortuneswell, the significance of which becomes clearer later.

From the Avalanche Church of St Andrew in Southwell the line continues south and terminates at a point on the coast called Longstone Ope, so named from a local tradition that a great fallen monolith once lay in the area. Maybe the purpose of this tall stone was to observe the

*Ordnance Survey Map cont'd.*

shortest shadow cast at noon on Midsummer's Day, or it may have been a marker for ancient mariners.

Between St George's Church and St John the Baptist's Church the meridian line passes through Tout Quarry near Priory Corner. A row of standing stones has recently been erected as a modern feature to the Tout Quarry Sculpture Park. They are oriented in the same north–south direction as the meridian, but not quite to the same axis. Local lore says a priory once stood on the edge of Tout Quarry, perhaps lost through a medieval landslip or quarrying.

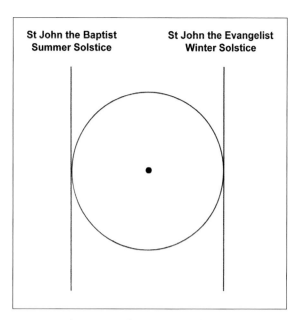

*Point within a circle with parallel lines of the two St John's.*

## The Pentagram

I found another alignment by plotting a line extending from the Primitive Methodist Chapel at Weston to the Catholic Church of St Andrew at the Grove passing through All Saints' Church in Easton.

As the diagram overleaf shows, this line is 36 degrees east of a line drawn from the Weston Chapel through the tower of St George's Church to the Jehovah's Witness Hall in Maidenwell. Knowing that this angle is associated with the five-sided figure called a pentagram, I followed my instincts by placing a protractor on St George's Church, drew a line of 72 degrees and found that it joined the other alignment on the south side of All Saints' Church, forming exactly one arm of a pentagram known as a 'golden triangle'. Curiously, the precise spot where the line from St George's meets the church of All Saints was until recently a lawn outside the south door, now the site of a new extension named the Millennium Wing.

The line from St George's to All Saints' also passes through the site of the Gospel Hall and along the frontage of the terraced houses on Reforne Street. The shorter side of the triangle, between St George's and All Saints', is proportionate to 1.618 of the longer sides radiating from Weston Chapel. This is the magic ratio referred to as the 'golden section'. This, like π (phi), was a mysterious ratio

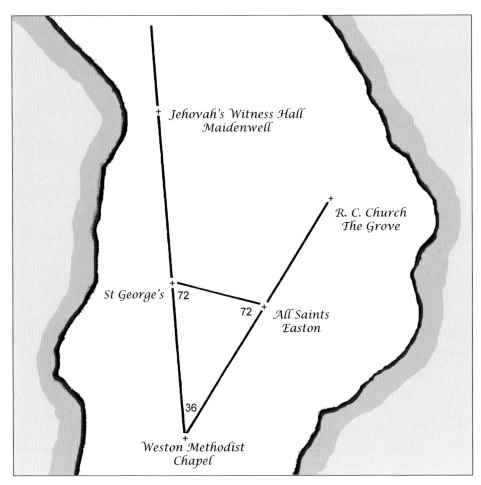

*The golden triangle.*

used by the ancient Egyptians and Greeks and later by the architects and artists of the Renaissance in their buildings, music, astronomy, poetry and paintings. Its purpose was primarily to create a pleasing and harmonious effect.

The Fibonacci series is a famous mathematical model of the golden section named after the thirteenth century Italian mathematician Fibonacci. His series of numbers 1, 2, 3, 5, 8, 13, 21, … can be found in the ratios and proportions of many natural patterns, such as the pads of a cat's paw, the arrangement of leaves on a plant and the spirals of a snail's shell.[2]

The early twentieth century Swiss pioneering architect Le Corbusier attempted a revival of this ancient proportion in the modern building design of the time using a 'modular' system based on the golden section. He claimed that the proportions of the perfect human form, standing 6 ft tall, embodied the golden section, and if buildings were constructed in accordance with these proportions, they would be both beautiful and well adapted to human needs.[3]

Using an accurate ruler and protractor, I extended the golden triangle to form a five-pointed star (pentagram). I was amazed at the number of now familiar churches placed on the lines of this geometric shape: St George's, the Methodist Church, now a Jehovah's Witness Kingdom Hall in Maidenwell, the Brackenbury Memorial Church at Fortuneswell, the church of Our Lady and St Andrew at the Grove, All Saints' Church at Easton, and the Primitive Methodist Chapel at Weston. When I joined the apexes to form the sides needed to create the shape of a pentagon, another former Methodist Church at Chesil near Mound Oel appeared, together with a former chapel in Weston, now a private house but once the site of the Oratory or Parsonage at Wakeham. A stone circle that once stood in the grounds of the Prison Governor's house may also have been included in this figure.

I then drew a line from All Saints' Church, situated between the lower legs of the pentagram, called the crux, to the northerly apex, the axis of the pentagram, which lies just behind the Police Station on the old Zig Zag Road.

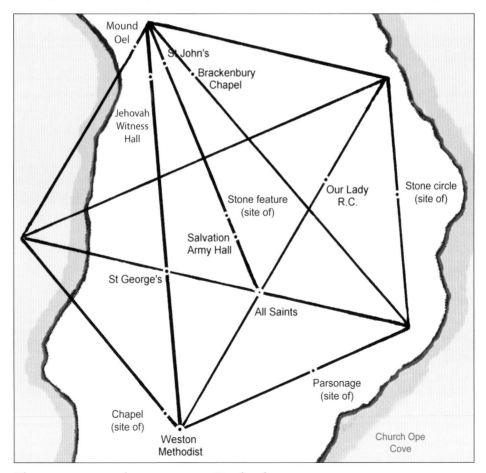

*The pentagram and pentagon over Portland.*

To my surprise, it passed through the Salvation Army Hall in Easton and St John the Baptist's Church in Fortuneswell. The exact centre of the figure is opposite the Drill Hall on Easton Lane, where ancient stones once stood in Victorian times. I calculated that seven churches and the old sites of the Priory and the Parsonage fall right on the lines of the completed geometry as well as the burial mound or barrow behind the old Driftwood Gallery at Chesil.

Strangely, only one of the arms of the pentagram incorporates a place of significance, the Primitive Methodist Chapel in Weston. The two eastern arms are in areas of scree called the Weares situated below the cliffs, the western arm reaches out into the sea by a third of a mile and the northern apex is on a housing estate on the old Zig Zag Road that leads to the Verne prison. At first this was disappointing; however, many of the lines of the pentagram feature far older sites such as stone circles and barrows. There is a possibility that ancient earthquakes and landslips, discussed earlier in the book, destroyed a building or monument sited on one of the eastern apexes. Alternatively, markers on the apexes may not be as crucial to the geometry as I thought, as it is the sacred distances and ratios between the churches that are the most significant aspect of this landscape design.

All Saints' Church at Easton with the zodiac ceiling, the 'Mark Point' referred to by King Warry, seems to be a key point on this figure, lying at the crux between the lower legs of the pentagram. Perhaps this site, like the others I have found on the island, was a site of ancient festivals. In fact, there is a clue in the dedication of the church. The festival of All Saints is held on 1 November, also known as All Hallows or Hallowmas ('hallows' meaning 'saints' and 'mas' meaning 'Mass'), a feast celebrated in honour of all the saints. The eve of All Hallows or Halloween is the day preceding it. The origin of the western festival of All Saints dates to 13 May AD 609 or 610 when Pope Boniface IV consecrated the Pantheon at Rome to the Blessed Virgin and all the martyrs; the feast of the 'dedicatio Sanctae Mariae ad Martyres' has been celebrated in Rome ever since. It continued to spread throughout Europe until the date of the festival was universally changed to 31 October by Pope Gregory III (AD 731–741). However, the Irish continued to maintain the original date of 1 November for many years after as the festival period of Samhain, a pre-Christian feast which honoured the dead as well as celebrated the Celtic New Year. The festival of Samhain later became a Christianised celebration of All Saints.

In many countries around Europe, All Saints' Day is celebrated by the lighting of candles and making offerings, such as flowers, to the dead. The 'Mark Point' may have once been a sacred site such as a barrow filled with the bones of the dead. King Warry writes of the importance of the old festivals on the island marking significant times of the year at specific places.

# St John the Baptist's Church

The Underhill parish church of St John the Baptist in Fortuneswell is one of the five major churches on Portland. Even though it does not feature in the Vesica geometry, its positioning on the axis of the pentagram as well as on the meridian line makes it significant.

*St John the Baptist's Church, Fortuneswell.*

Built in 1839, St John's Church established by the Church of England provided a place of worship urgently needed for the Underhill community after the decline of St George's Church. The site chosen was so steep that a foundation platform had to be built into the hillside, giving the church an unusual south–east orientation instead of the usual Christian east–west. The situation of the high altar in the sanctuary is curious; it is placed higher than the main body of the church. According to the warden, the reason for this is a mystery. Perhaps the raised platform stands on the foundations of an earlier building. King Warry refers to local objections to the building of this church:

> *"... much opposition, and a curse was laid on the church and whoever officiated as vicar – by whom and of what nature exactly I do not remember, but curiously enough up to recent times the church has not had a happy history in one way or another, and I have often heard the old curse referred to in jest or earnest."*[4]

According to Peter E.G. Harvey, Captain Manning of Portland Castle laid the foundation stone and dedicated the church to St John the Baptist, after a chapel in the Tower of London.[5] This is probably another tall tale as the chapel in the White Tower, one of the oldest in England, is dedicated to St John the Evangelist. St John the Baptist, however, is the original Patron of Freemasonry, significant to the stonemasons, the old Guilds and secret societies.

*The leaded west window of St John the Baptist's Church, showing the geometric squared circle.*

The position of St John the Baptist's Church on the geometry is also interesting and symbolic, it being the most northerly church on the island and situated within the head of the pentagram on its main axis. The ancient order of the Knights Templars worshipped an image of the Baptist's head and dedicated many of their churches to this saint.

The church has some interesting features and symbolism. The leaded design of the west window above the high altar is curiously different from the others, depicting a geometric squared circle. The position of this window is significant as it permits the sun to cast a shadow of the squared circle over the altar during the height of summer, around the feast day of St John the Baptist. The eastern leaded window of Rosslyn Chapel near Edinburgh, a sanctuary considered by many to contain Templar secrets, also shines the image of the mystical squared circle over the altar, symbolic of the earth body (square) and the spirit (circle). In sacred geometry the square is static and symbolises the material or physical plane, while the circle symbolises the spiritual plane or the heavenly realms. The squared circle represents the union of spirit and matter.

*Rose window of St John the Baptist's Church.*

St John's Church also boasts a beautiful rose window above the altar depicting mystical scenes in stained glass of the Crucifixion and Resurrection. One window depicts Christ with Mary Magdalene in the Garden of Gethsemane, with an angel appearing in the top corner presenting the Holy Grail.

# An Ancient Symbol of Divine Proportion

Because the pentagram has occult associations, I wondered if the landscape pentagram I had found held a more sinister connotation as regards Portland's links with witchcraft. However, I found that the true meaning of the pentagram was in fact very sacred and spiritual. John Michell describes the pentagram as being associated with humanity, seen as the human body with arms outstretched and legs apart. He writes:

> *"The associated God was Hermes, the medium of revelation and keeper of mysteries. Christian mystics made the pentagram an emblem of Jesus, who divided five loaves to feed five thousand people and who represents the archetypal man (with five senses and five fingers to each hand)."*[7]

The human figure in the pentagram known as the Vitruvian Man, made famous by Leonardo da Vinci, reflects the divine proportions of man within the ratio of the body parts. For example, the distance from the top of your head to the ground is proportional to the distance from your belly button to the ground by 1.618. This measure also equates to the building blocks of DNA and is the divine blueprint of life, love and beauty. People surrounded by measure that conflicts with the golden section are living out of harmony and balance with their environment.

The medieval stonemasons who built the Gothic cathedrals around Europe also used the pentagram in their designs, as it is the greatest expression of the golden section. The five-pointed figure also characterises the planet Venus and the path she takes across the heavens during an 8-year cycle. According to my findings, five seems to be a key number on Portland: a five-sided figure in the landscape marked by churches, five main towns with five ancient symbols marked on a Reeve staff, five island saints, five main churches and a five-sided castle that had during the nineteenth century 50 steps leading down to the ruins of St Andrew's.

References to temples of Venus on Portland gave me the idea that the island may have been a centre for the worship of the planet or the goddess Venus. Ancient descriptions of Venus refer to "a star that smoked"[8] or as having a beard and horns, suggesting that the planet may not have always appeared as it does today. Long ago, in an age when skies were clearer, the situation of Portland jutting out from the south coast would have greatly enhanced the viewing of

Venus. The ancient megalithic priests would have been able to observe her spectacular risings and settings into and out of the sea, marking them with stones to calculate her cycles over the years.

This knowledge may have continued with the later Druids, who depicted the upside-down crescent horn of Venus (as seen in her moon-like phases) on standing stones. With today's polluted atmosphere, it is difficult to see the crescent Venus without using binoculars. Artemis, Ishtar, Anath and Isis are all horned deities associated with this planet and I wondered if the Ancients also considered the horned shape of Portland sacred to this planet.

Besides the Venus temple traditionally believed to be at Church Ope Cove as King Warry records, there may have been others on Portland. The famous Dorset author Thomas Hardy wrote, "... tradition urged that a temple to Venus once stood at the top of the Roman road leading up into the isle; and possibly one to the love-goddess of the Slingers antedated this".[9] (By 'slingers' Hardy was referring to Portland's earliest inhabitants.) Archaeologists unearthed a tessellated pavement of a possible Roman temple or villa in Belle Vue Terrace, Fortuneswell. The Avalanche Church of St Andrew in Southwell may have been the site of another temple as pieces of a similar pavement were found near the church.

There is another significant alignment on Portland with a Masonic influence, linking St Andrew's Church at Church Ope Cove with the Millennium pillars in Victoria Square at the entrance to Portland. These columns were carved to look like beacons, erected as the 'Gate to Portland'. Other sites on this line include the ancient Oratory or Parsonage, the Bible Christian Chapel in Wakeham, now destroyed, the Parish Church of All Saints and another Methodist chapel at the bottom of the High Street in Chesil. The line also passes alongside the Masonic Hall before going through the pillars.

The two pillars are a significant Masonic symbol found in all Masonic Lodges around the world, representing the ancient pillars that guarded Solomon's Temple. Masonic scholars believe that the pillars of Solomon's Temple were freestanding, symbolic of the twin aspects or male/female polarity of the deity. The builder of the temple, the Phoenician Hiram Abif, may have copied them from his home city of Tyre, where reportedly two pillars stood at the entrance to the Temple of Hercules 'fashioned of gold and emerald'. The inclusion of the Masonic Hall and the twin pillars on a line to the old mother church of St Andrew at Church Ope Cove seems to support my theory that Freemasonic knowledge is responsible for some of the alignments and geometry on the island.

The distance that separates the churches or the radius of the circle, as mentioned in Chapter 4, is approximately 0.85 of a mile. The diameter of the circle is therefore 1.7 miles. The radius is close to an ancient Greek mile of 1,388 m or 0.8626 of an English mile. Why the Portlanders chose such a measure between the churches has so far eluded me. However, the closeness to the ancient Greek mile may suggest some foreign influence from the Mediterranean.

These intriguing facts and discoveries spurred me towards my next quest, to discover more about the old Portland families and their origins, whose knowledge may have contributed to these mysterious landscape figures.

*The Gate to Portland.*

# Chapter 7

# The Legacy of the Sea Peoples

Ancient British history is the subject of much speculation by many academic historians. The earliest descriptions of Britain and its inhabitants cannot be wholly trusted because the majority of the information comes from people who either sought to conquer the island or held political or religious agendas. Sometimes a glimmer of truth can emerge from the history handed down to us over the generations through oral traditions. However, they too are open to interpretation. Archaeologists are often conventional, relying on more logical and scientific theories. Today, it is imperative that the researcher takes a much wider and more common-sense approach, using every resource available.

The old Portlanders recall the earliest name of their isle as Vindilis or Vindilia, a Latin name meaning Fortress Island, a suitable description considering the topography. According to the oral traditions, their earliest ancestors, 'the Ancients', inhabited the Verne hillfort and built many of the earthworks around the island. Thomas Hardy in his novel *The Well Beloved* refers to them as 'Slingers'. This name derives from an old Portland tradition that the original settlers on Portland could accurately throw perfectly rounded Chesil Beach stones with a leather strap from the cliffs at any invaders; excavations at the Verne have uncovered many of these sling stones or rounded pebbles.

The Slingers are also described as a race of tall people.[1] This may have been corrupted into the often-told tale that the devil or a giant played quoits from Portland Pike (Yeates roundabout) where he threw a large stone that landed below the place that is now occupied by a chimney-type tower east of Abbotsbury called Hardy's Monument. The thrown stone is actually the capstone of a Neolithic dolmen called the Hellstone, just below Hardy's Monument.[2] Further west of the Monument is the Valley of Stones, strewn with boulders supposedly left by the quoit-playing giants. In the folklore of southwest Britain, there are many locations associated with either the devil or a giant throwing large stones or playing quoits (when Christianity swept through the area, the devil replaced the giant in some of the stories).[3]

Walking east from The Heights Hotel towards the Verne Citadel (1860–1887) you can see the great ditches that form the defences of the fort built by convicts. These defences, though Victorian, are a reminder of its long-forgotten history as a single- or possibly a double-banked hillfort, dating from the Iron Age (1000–50 BC), enclosing an area of about an acre. This site, once a beacon hill, is the highest point on Portland with unobstructed views over the harbour and mainland, ideal as a lookout for invaders from the sea.

Between 4000 and 1000 BC, incorporating the Neolithic and Bronze Ages, an advanced culture (known as the Wessex Culture) farmed the chalk plains of southern England, an area later called Wessex by the Saxons. The ancient boundaries of this Bronze Age 'Garden of England' were the Rivers Axe in Devon, the Avon at Christchurch and the northern Avon at Bath. The Wessex Culture built Avebury and Stonehenge within their realm, the greatest and largest stone temples in Europe, and massive sculptured earthen mounds such as Silbury Hill. Also included are the lesser-known stone circles of Stanton Drew south of Bristol, one of which is the second largest stone circle in England. In Dorset they built the great 7-mile cursus (processional avenue) near Cranborne and the mysterious circular earthworks and mounds north of Wimborne at Knowlton.

From archaeological evidence, the ancient inhabitants of Wessex were also great seafarers and traders who travelled to the Mediterranean and the Baltic Seas from their main ports below Hengistbury Head near Christchurch at the mouth of the Avon and from Melcombe Regis opposite Portland. Portland's geographical position could not fail to make it important to the Wessex Culture whose contact with foreign civilisations is undeniable. It is a fact that many of the small islands around the south coast of Britain were places of barter and trade from at least the Iron Age. Because of its strategic location and its reputation as a safe and secure haven, Portland was very likely a major trading centre between the wealthy merchants on the mainland and the sea peoples coming from northern Europe and the Mediterranean, particularly if the mainland suffered from local disputes and tribal wars.

One of the most tumultuous periods of unrest occurred between 145 and 72 BC, just before the first Roman invasions; as many as 26 British kings ruled consecutively over a period of 73 years, many of them reigning for only 2 years (see Appendix B).

# The Druids

Portland folklore recalls the mysterious Druids who sacrificed at stone altars and circles near the Grove. In the past, historians have held the view that the Druids were unholy pagans, superior magicians and sorcerers lusting for sacrifice and blood. This was undoubtedly political propaganda used by the Romans before their invasion, for, in truth, Druidism was the centre and source from which radiated the whole system of organised civil and ecclesiastical knowledge, and it was practised throughout the British Isles. Members of its order acted as diplomats, legislators, priests, physicians, lawyers, teachers and poets.[4] They used a prehistoric system of memorising events, facts and history into groups of three poems called Triads.

*The Welsh Triads*, one of the earliest books of British history, records that the first Druids arrived from the sea with Hu Gadarn Hysicion, or Hu the Mighty. This great man led the first migrations of the Kymry from Defrobane, the ancient name for Constantinople, during the Bronze Age around 1800 BC. Hu is described as one of the "Three Benefactors of the Race of the Kymry", one of the "Three Primary Sages of his adopted land" and one of the "Three Pillars of the Race of the Island of Britain".[5] A few miles east of Portland on the coast near Lulworth is Kimmeridge (ridge of the Kymry).

The British regarded Hu as the personification of intellect and culture, who promoted agriculture and obtained lands not by forfeiture and contention but through 'equality and in peace'. The Welsh documents commemorate him for inventing *The Triads*, "having made poetry the vehicle of memory and record".[6] Hu also established a Gorsedd, an assembly of Druids and Bards, who often performed in an open grass clearing conspicuous and audible to all people.[7] Just north of Portland near Dorchester is Maiden Castle, one of the largest hillforts in the world, where Druids still assemble today.

Aedd Mawr (*c* 1200 BC), a descendant of Hu, is reputed to be the founder of the Druidical Order in Britain. He entrusted three wise men called Plenydd, Alawn and Gwron with the work of organising his dominions, and they established three orders, the Druids, Bards and Ovates. In Britain, the order of the Druids had 31 seats of education; the primary colleges were Caer Troia in London, Caer Evroc in York and Caer Leon in Caerleon near Newport in Wales.[6]

Julius Caesar, the Roman General who invaded Britain, knew of the Druids. He wrote:

> "It is believed that the rule of life was discovered in Britain and to have spread thence to Gaul and today those who would study the subject more accurately journey, as a rule, to Britain to learn it."[8]

Pliny (AD 23–79) is more specific:

> "At the present time, Britannia is fascinated by magic and performs its rites with so much ceremony that it would seem as though it was she who imparted the cult to the Persians."[9]

From the many stones found around the country that display Druidical art, we can deduce that they made use of symbols as communication. The circle was most sacred to them, symbolising their belief in reincarnation, of life without end. Other symbols easily recognised as theirs relate to astrology, a science they understood well. Druidic knowledge of the planets was far in advance of most other countries; they even carved upon their stones the image of the upside-down crescent horn of Venus, as seen in its moon-like phases not visible to the naked eye.

In the days before Christianity, the British were skilled sailors, with ships far superior to those of the Romans in their size and manoeuvrability. With their knowledge of the constellations, they could travel great distances to islands off the coast of Britain and beyond. Sacred to the Druids were the islands of Orkney, Iona, the Isle of Man, Anglesey, the Isle of Wight and the Scilly Isles, where, protected by the sea, they performed magic and ceremony in honour of their gods. These islands were mystical realms of the dead, particularly those with causeways like Portland and St Michael's Mount in Cornwall which allowed access for mortals to worship their deities and honour their dead with festivals on sacred days of the solar and lunar year. The old pagan festival sites on Portland continue to be remembered in the dedication of the new churches to the saints whose feast days fall close to or on these celebrated days.

*The Triads* of the early Welsh Bards refer to the Isle of Wight as one of three principal islands sacred to the Druids.[5] Local folklore tells of the Druids sacrificing white bulls at the Mottistone, a megalithic stone on the downs. On the eastern tip near Bembridge they worshipped in a grove, honouring the full moon as it rose out of the sea.[10] Locals still refer to this place as 'Moon Grove', a place where white-robed priests symbolically captured the silvery light of the moon in their sacred precinct. The name Grove on Portland may also have derived from its association with the Druids and their worship of the moon. Elizabeth Pearce recalled that the first rays of the full moon in winter bathe the island at the Grove from behind St Alban's Head.[1]

A little stone chapel dedicated to St Aldhelm (a nephew of King Ine) stands as a seamark on St Alban's Head, built within a circular henge, part of which is still visible. This may have been an ancient precinct of the Druids aligned to the Grove. A local person has observed that from the chapel, the sun at the equinox sets behind Verne Hill on the highest part of Portland.[11]

Today Portland has no recorded history or archaeological evidence relating to the Druids. Local folklore and place names such as the Grove and Paradise are the only remnants of this time that keep alive the memory of their sacred precincts for future generations to either contemplate or dismiss, sadly mostly the latter.

# The Veneti and the Morini

During the nineteenth century, unusual beehive chambers were uncovered during quarrying, some of which had connecting passages.[12] Although archaeologists believe these to be storage chambers for grain that date from the Iron Age, some of the finds, such as pottery, bones and ritual objects, predate the Iron Age. Their construction and corbelled ceilings resemble some of the Celtic monastic settlements found in Ireland or the Tholos tombs in Greece. Unfortunately, nobody preserved any of these mysterious structures, as at the time excavation would have created expensive delays for the contractors. I recall a story told to me by an old Portlander about an underground-pillared crypt discovered by accident under playing fields near the Grove. Apparently, archaeologists did a quick survey and determined it to be an ancient water reservoir, and the council filled it with concrete the next day.

In Dorset, the Iron Age tribes built the most impressive ancient defences in Britain, the greatest of which was Maiden Castle. A pre-Roman route from this hillfort follows the Wey River valley to Portland. Iron Age settlers left their mark on Portland at other places besides the Verne hillfort; they also enclosed settlements with earthworks at Southwell and Blacknor halfway down the western side of the island. The reason for such elaborate defences on such a small island remains a mystery, as no local records from that period survive.

According to some Roman and medieval historians, two of the early tribes who helped refortify Dorset were the Morini and the Veneti; both names mean 'sea people'. The Veneti may be the early ancestors of the Slovenians who settled in central Europe on their migrations from Asia Minor. The Greek historians Homer and Strabo refer to the Veneti as living in an area near Troy and Paphlagonia in Asia Minor, before the Trojan War.[13] They later established themselves in the north-east region of Italy and Slovenia, from Trieste on the shore of the Adriatic to the mouth of the River Po. These Veneti are also descended from the Illyrians who were Aryan Indo-Europeans. Other areas the Veneti have settled include the far north-east of present-day Estonia, and Brittany.[14] The Roman general Julius Caesar wrote:

> "These Veneti exercise by far the most extensive authority over all the sea-coast in those districts, for they have numerous ships, in which it is their custom to sail to Britain, and they excel the rest in the theory and practice of navigation."

> "For their ships were built and equipped after this manner. The keels were somewhat flatter than those of our ships, whereby they could more easily encounter the shallows and the ebbing of the tide: the prows were raised

*very high, and, in like manner the sterns were adapted to the force of the waves and storms. The ships were built wholly of oak, and designed to endure any force and violence whatever; the benches which were made of planks a foot in breadth, were fastened by iron spikes of the thickness of a man's thumb; the anchors were secured fast by iron chains instead of cables, and for sails they used skins and thin dressed leather."*[8]

L.A. Waddell wrote that the prehistoric aboriginal race called the Van, originating from Armenia in the area around Lake Van, were ancestors of the Veneti.[15] Many academics believe the Celts came from this area, leading some to believe that the Veneti were a Celtic tribe. The Romans called many of the earlier Celtic settlements names that began with Vin, such as Vindaclava, the name for Badbury Rings near Wimborne, and Vindilia, the ancient name for Portland. The Veneti worshipped a sun god they called Belin, similar to Belennos or Beli, the sun god of the Gauls. Sarah Pearce refers to the island soldiery in ancient times as the Portland 'Belenes or Slingers'.[16] Robert Pearce mentions they were called by these names as far back as the year AD 837.[17] The Veneti were also renowned as great stone slingers.

The Morini tribe, another seafaring race, lived in the area between the Rivers Rhine and Seine. They formed an alliance with the Veneti against the Romans and many came to Dorset when Gaul (now France and northern Germany) fell to the Romans. Wareham, the next major port along the coast east of Portland, received its most ancient name of 'Morinio' from this tribe.

Nehalennia was their tribal goddess, a deity later worshipped by British sailors. The remaining Veneti and Morini fleets may have found refuge in Ireland away from the Romans, who never seriously invaded the Emerald Isle. Settlers, recorded in ancient Irish annals as the Moran, may be the same race of people.

Some of the Veneti and the Morini merged with the local inhabitants of ancient Dorset called the Durotriges. Hutchins believed they refortified the hilltop enclosures of Dorset and ruled over Wessex.[18] The Romans regarded the Durotriges, meaning 'a tribe who dwells by water', as the fiercest of the British tribes. The slinging skills of the Veneti must have been a great asset to the Durotriges.

I noticed from the study of folklore in Britain and Europe that places associated with giants also have traditions of a race of seafaring traders called the Phoenicians. The early chronicles of Ireland refer to its oldest race of people as very tall, fierce and religious warriors called the Fomorians, also meaning 'sea peoples'. They built great stone sanctuaries on the western side of Ireland that still survive today. Some historians believe they were the Amorite Phoenicians, the giants of biblical fame whom Moses and Joshua endeavoured to destroy.[15]

# The Phoenicians

From at least 3000 BC, the Phoenicians were nomadic seafaring traders who ruled the Mediterranean Sea and beyond from a narrow strip of land we now call Syria. The great city-states of Phoenicia ended with the fall of Tyre to the Babylonian king Nebuchadnezzar in 573 BC and later to Alexander the Great in 332 BC. According to Greek historians, Phoenicians traded with Britain for metals such as copper, tin and lead, and a Phoenician gold coin was unearthed during the building of the Verne prison.[19] Pytheas, a travelling Greek from Marseilles, visited Britain on a voyage around 330 BC.[22] His mission was to investigate the rumours of a lucrative trade in tin, exclusively controlled by the Phoenicians, and to divert some of this trade across land through Europe. Tin was in great demand by many ancient cultures for mixing with copper to make bronze tools and weapons. The Phoenicians were aware that Cornwall had the largest deposits of tin in Europe and the trading of this metal increased their wealth and power in the Mediterranean. Among the exhibits inside Portland Museum are two pre-Roman iron ingots discovered whilst excavating the Verne prison. The Phoenicians and the Veneti used iron ingots as currency for trade.

*Iron ingots, Portland Museum.*

Dorset's natural harbours and chalk downs were clear of the heavy forestation that hindered overland travel through Devon and Hampshire. Consequently, there are many recognised Bronze Age routes across Dorset to many ancient centres around the country. One researched trade route ran between Portland and Porlock in Somerset,[23] while another links Portland with the old port of Bristol. Both these routes were built for valuable overland trade such as gold from Ireland; Bronze Age Irish gold has been found in Dorset's burial mounds.

It is possible that the transportation of Cornish tin came overland to the safer and more convenient harbour of Portland. The little port of Morlaix on the north coast of France directly opposite Portland received the tin from Britain for overland transportation to Marseilles for onward shipping to Mediterranean ports. Ancient mariners often preferred to stay as near to the coast as possible and shorten the journey wherever practicable. The situation of Portland jutting out into the Channel with its natural harbour of the Mere would have made the island ideal for those with valuable cargo. This almost impregnable island would have been a perfect place to store their commodities or even trade with the British. In addition, the crossing from Weymouth to Cherbourg or Morlaix is almost certain to have been the more convenient route for shipment across the English Channel to Gaul.

The Phoenicians were not only great traders of metals but also skilled in stone masonry. They built massive stone temples around Europe and the Middle East without mortar, using sacred geometry within their design. The finest example of their achievements is Baalbek in the Lebanon, a temple that contains the largest cut stones in the world. The magnificent city of Carthage with its central canal should have been one of the wonders of the ancient world. Perhaps some of the great empires of Europe and the Middle East hired the Phoenician master stonemasons to build their magnificent temples and cities, as in the case of Hiram Abif, the Phoenician who built the famous biblical Solomon's Temple in Jerusalem. The Phoenicians, as great stonemasons, knew the value of good building stone. They may have been the first race to quarry Portland stone, and, after settling on the island, could have imparted their knowledge of sacred geometry to the local inhabitants.

## Place Name Associations

Phoenicians worshipped the sun god Baal, also known as Beale and later Bel, similar to the Veneti. They honoured their god by conducting fire ceremonies on hilltops and by using natural features such as rock pinnacles as altars. I felt that if Portland was indeed an important harbour for this race, perhaps signs of their religious practices might still survive. Research revealed place names on Portland such as Beals Croft, a field near Southwell, and the Beal, an earlier name for the southerly point now called the Bill, a site where the inhabitants once venerated the Phoenician sun god Baal. The island has celebrated the Celtic spring festival of Bel-tane for centuries, including midsummer, when locals leapt through the flames of bonfires lit on the Beal (Bill) in a ritual that could be seen as a continuation of some ancestral ceremony.[24]

A few miles north of Portland on the downs near Cerne Abbas in Dorset is the Cerne Giant, a large ancient chalk-cut hill figure of a naked man wielding a club. Some antiquarians believe in the tradition that the giant represented Melkart Hercules (Melcarth), the first Phoenician King of Tyre who defeated Albion to become ruler of Britain.[25] Remarkably, the destruction of Tyre, the great island port of the Phoenicians, by Alexander the Great is an event still recalled by nineteenth century Portlanders.[26] According to Beaumont, Portland has geographical similarities with ancient Tyre, as both are separated from the mainland by a narrow channel and each have a sacred high place. Melcarth was a Phoenician god of the city of Tyre and called by the Greeks the Phoenician Hercules. He was often depicted holding a staff in each hand, identical to the Long Man of Wilmington, a hill figure on the Sussex Downs. Beaumont also states that the Dorset place names of Melcombe and Melbury encapsulate the god Melcarth.[26] My research of the name revealed a biblical king called Melek, a giant of the seafaring Ammorites, ancestors of the Phoenicians known to originate from northern Israel. A temple to Melcarth was also uncovered in Carthage.

The Phoenicians, like the Druids, were worshippers of the constellations whose deity was Astarte, 'Queen of the Sky'. She is the wife of Baal and referred to as the moon goddess. Her sisters were Asherah and Anath, the goddess Venus. Astarte is also associated with swans, which have nested at the end of Chesil Beach below the village of Abbotsbury for centuries. A chapel to St Catherine, Astarte's Christianised counterpart, stands upon a sculptured terraced hill above Abbotsbury.[27] A future archaeological excavation around the chapel may reveal an earlier shrine.

## Associations with St Andrew and St George

According to researchers such as L.A. Waddell, the crosses of St Andrew and St George are Phoenician in origin and the saints themselves are Christianised gods that have their roots in prehistory.[15] Along the Phoenician trading routes of the Baltic, from Scotland to Russia, we find many islands and countries that adopted Andrew and George as their patron saints.

*Indara from a Hittite seal (note the cross of St Andrew on his head).*

Because St Andrew was portrayed as a fisherman in Biblical texts, many people came to view him as the patron saint of fishermen. However, Jesus called upon him to be a disciple with the words "come, follow me, and I will make you fishers of men".[28] Waddell claims that the name Andrew is not Hebrew like many of the other saints, but Aryan–Phoenician. Indara was the father-god of the eastern branch of the Aryan Barats, so Andrew could be a derivation of Indaru (Indara) from ancient Sumeria. One tablet describes Indara (Andrew) thus:

> *"O Lord Indara thou sturdy director of men*
> *Thou makest the multitude to dwell in peace"*
>
> *"Indara leader of heavenly hosts and human races!*
> *Indara encompassed the Dragon*
> *O Light winner day's creator"*[15]

The use and worship of St Andrew's cross, the 'X' cross, was widespread in ancient Britain and depicted on many early British coins and in Phoenician art. Unlike the early Christian equal-armed cross, it tilts to project protection or defence. A Hittite seal from 2000 BC depicts the X cross on the head of Indara as he is about to slay the dragon, similar to his western counterpart, St George.

The earliest depictions of the equal-armed cross of St George are on prehistoric Hittite and Sumerian seals. Many Phoenician coins depict the cross within a circle which was believed to represent fire and the sun; one coin shows their goddess of the seas, Baratti, who sits upon a throne incorporating a cross within a circle, resembling the figure of our Britannia.

*Phoenician coins depicting Baratti. (Taken from* The Phoenician Origins of Britons, Scots and Anglo-Saxons *by L. Waddell, with kind permission of The Banton Press.)*

The red (fire) cross on a white background is supposed to originate with St George, the patron saint of England, famed by the crusaders. His beginnings are rooted in medieval fictions; some historians say he was a warrior from Cappadocia in Turkey, part of the Hittite empire.[15]

## Coffins and Stone Heads: A Clue to Portland's Phoenician Heritage

Over 300 unusual carved limestone coffins or sarcophagi, said to be Romano-British, have been unearthed on Portland at the Grove, Verne Common and many of the quarries. Some luckily escaped destruction by quarrymen and now reside in the garden of Portland Museum in Wakeham. During my first visit to the museum, I examined the coffins and found them to be unlike the usual coffins ascribed to the Romans.

*One of many sarcophagi found on Portland, said to be Roman.*

*Sixth century BC Etruscan sarcophagus.*

Shortly afterwards, I travelled to Baratti Archaeological Park near Piombino in central Italy. Although I was intrigued by Etruscan culture, it was the name that fascinated me, for Baratti, as mentioned earlier, is a Phoenician name for their sea goddess. (The Etruscans allowed the Phoenicians to have their own port which they named Baratti after their own goddess.) The Italians regard this archaeological site as highly important. The guide then took me to another part of the cemetery where lay several freestanding stone sarcophagi identical to those I had seen in the garden of the Portland Museum. The guide explained that these coffins date from the sixth century BC and were produced for the middle classes, mainly foreigners such as Greeks and Italic peoples. I asked if they might be the tombs of seafarers from distant lands, such as the Phoenicians, and the guide agreed. I believe that Baratti, like Portland, was a Phoenician colony and a cemetery for their dead.

L.A. Waddell states that the name Britannia derives from the combining of the Phoenician sea goddess 'Barat' with 'Anna', the prehistoric goddess of the aboriginal Britons.[15] One of the field names on Portland is Parrates Acre, which may be another reminder of this great seafaring race; the P and B interchangeable in the old languages gives us Barrates Acre.

Also in the museum garden is an unusual stone head by the side of one of the sarcophagus. Upon enquiry, an attendant at the museum informed me that a local had discovered the head buried in his garden and used it as a garden ornament. However, it began to receive a lot of unwanted attention when Portlanders started to bow to it as they passed by. Eventually, it was donated to the museum.

The sculpture has an unusual presence and appears to have either a helmeted headdress or a Mohican hairstyle. The face has a likeness to those I have seen carved on the walls of Egyptian temples said to depict the invading sea peoples, a race many consider Phoenician. The eyes of the Portland head are slanted and oriental in appearance, similar to the early depictions of the Etruscans of Italy I had seen in museums. It also has a large crooked Semitic-looking nose and a long pointed beard.

The head is made of granite, not local limestone. This makes the carving even more remarkable because of the skill involved in cutting and shaping this hard crystalline rock. Carved stone human heads have been unearthed in many areas of Britain and Ireland, including islands such as Anglesey, in the northwest of Wales and on the Isle of Man. Many religious groups, from the ancient Celts to the Knights Templars, have practised the mysterious 'Cult of the Head', a form of worship using an idol of a head fashioned in stone. It is possible that the early inhabitants of Portland once worshipped the head, particularly if Bran is associated with the island. Other Celtic stone heads found on Portland are cruder than this one, and are also on display in the Portland Museum.

*Mysterious stone head found buried on Portland, now in the Portland Museum.*

# The Heritage of the Old Portland Families

In the book *Angels, Cherubim, and Gods*, the author makes a remark about Portland locals:

> *"The inhabitants who say that they are Phoenicians have never, until lately, allowed any English, or 'foreigners', as they term us, to hold land in their territory, but have kept themselves a distinct people."*[20]

Elizabeth Pearce refers to a local tradition concerning the early occupants of Portland:

> *"The first group were the Combens, descendants of the Phoenicians, who still live on the island, and they recall the name of the Mediterranean colony from whence they came."*[1]

Comben is a Celtic name derived from 'Combe' or 'valley' (hence Combe-valley men). The valley leading downwards to Chiswell also has Celtic names such as Maidenwell and Branscombe. Local tradition refers to this area of the island as the first place of dwelling.

The Mediterranean colony from where the Combens first originated might be one of the Balearic Islands off the south coast of Spain, which include Ibiza, Mallorca and Menorca. In ancient times, stone slinging was a unique skill particular to the inhabitants of these islands. The Balearics were once Phoenician territory, and the name derives from the Phoenician word 'Bal jaro' meaning a 'master at slinging'.[21] Even the Romans referred to these islanders as excellent slingers. Carthaginian sailors, from the North African Empire of the western Phoenicians, whose great city was Carthage, in present-day Tunisia, supposedly discovered Britain in 500 BC. Their nearly successful attack on Rome led by General Hannibal was partly due to the accuracy of their frontline stone slingers from the Balearics.

The Comben family may be descendants of the Veneti, the dominant seafaring force throughout Europe in the Iron Age and a branch of the western Phoenicians. The Romans defeated the Veneti fleet, possibly capturing survivors and imprisoning them on Portland; the island is certainly geographically suited for this purpose even today.

The Pearce family were the second race of people to arrive and settle on Portland after the Combens. According to locals, they originated from Ireland and came over via Cornwall. It is quite likely they were the Celtic Christian missionaries sent from Ireland to reintroduce the early Christian teaching that came out of the Holy Land shortly after the Crucifixion. Dorset has many ancient links with Ireland; for example, Wimborne Minster in Dorset retains part of a round tower, built by Irish missionaries in Saxon times, that stood separate from the church.[29] One line of research links the name Pearce with Normandy, as many with that name came to Britain with William the Conqueror in 1066. Elizabeth Pearce recalls that they were the second family to settle on Portland before the Whites. The White family settled on the island around AD 720; therefore the arrival of the Pearce clan had to be before this date and after the Roman occupation, probably during the fifth or sixth century when records show that Irish missionaries visited Dorset. Free from Roman and Saxon invasion, Ireland became a safe haven for Iron Age sea peoples and early Christians. Their history records invasions from the Celtic Greeks, namely the Nemedians, Parthenon and the Tuatha De Dannan; many Irish ports have Phoenician names beginning with Bal or Bally derived from their sun god Baal.

The Reeve staffs in the Portland Museum gave me another clue to the ancient cultures on Portland. I found that there are five different mystic symbols carved on the staffs, each representing a village. The symbol V represents Chiswell, VV Easton, X Weston, O Southwell, and a cross within a circle Wakeham and Church Ope Cove. A search through books on the ancient symbols and languages of the world revealed that one of them included all these symbols – this was the Proto Phoenician script. The ancient Norse used a notched stick called a Skor to keep track of numerical information, which is where we get the word 'score'.[30] The Reeve staff's origins could be more ancient. John Udal refers to it as "This mode of holding land, which the inhabitants, who have no title deeds, affirm to have been from time immemorial, is evidently of Eastern origin and early date".[31] The *Old Testament* refers to a similar custom in Ezekiel (37:16), where marks made on a stick represented the tribes of Israel. This information led me to discover the origins and remarkable legacy of the third family to settle on Portland – the Whites.

Research at Dorchester Library revealed a most intriguing tradition concerning the Whites, whose origins I discovered were Jutish. Anglo-Saxon King Ine of Wessex invited 120 of them to colonise Portland, being near relatives with the same noble blood. They were to settle alongside the existing inhabitants as equals, choosing to live in the area now called Wakeham, with its own access to the sea at Church Ope Cove. They brought with them the custom of Gavelkind, which continued on Portland up until Victorian times. Gavelkind refers to the ancient practice of dividing one's estate amongst all your children, sons and daughters alike. This was in complete contrast to the English custom of leaving the estate to the eldest son. Gavelkind ensured that the women of the island were able to enjoy financial freedom without the need to marry.[1] I discovered that this ancient practice was in use in other parts of England settled by the Jutes.

# King Ine

According to *The Anglo-Saxon Chronicle*,[32] Ine, born around AD 650, was the son of King Coenred of Dorset, whose ancestor Cerdic (died AD 534) was a Jute and first king of Wessex.[33] As the son of a Dorset King, Ine most probably spent many years as a child living in this area and acquired the manor of Portland when he became King of Wessex in 688. The *Chronicle* further states that in 694 he became the second Anglo-Saxon king after Ethelbert of Kent to issue a written code of laws, a moral code that Alfred the Great continued. This, historians say, changed the nature of administration in Wessex and did a great deal to centralise the kingdom, laying the foundations for a later united Britain ruled over by one king.[34] Even the name Ine suggests unification, as 'one' in the old Welsh language sounds like 'In'.

Ine was probably acquainted with the qualities of Portland stone, as he was the first king to order stone building since the Romans. Welsh records and traditions say he instructed the building of the first stone church at Glastonbury, just west of the wooden holy church allegedly founded by early Christians.[35] The first Minster in the City of Winchester, built over a Druidic temple, was another of his many achievements. He founded or possibly revived an order of stonemasons to help build these religious buildings, hiring master masons from France, the Holy Land, or even the Phoenician descendants of Portland. I began to wonder why the Kings of Britain jealously guarded Portland for themselves. Was it to keep safe the inhabitants who held this ancient knowledge of building with sacred geometry?

In 726 King Ine, nearing the end of his life, abdicated his throne and travelled on a pilgrimage to Rome, like his predecessor King Caedwalla. Aethelburgh, his Saxon queen, was a devout Roman Catholic and probably persuaded him to make the journey. One tradition says that in Rome Ine and his wife watched and prayed at the tomb of the Apostles in the guise of poor and pious pilgrims. In the district known as Burges Saxonum (modern Borgo), Ine founded a hospice or home for English pilgrims. Some historians trace the foundation of the English College in Rome back to this hospice. In 728 Ine died, blessing God that he and his wife had been allowed to lay their dust in the consecrated soil of Rome. The memory of the hospice still lives in the Church of San Spirito in Sassia, formerly Santa Maria in Saxia, now the district of Borgo within the Vatican walls. Here Ine lies entombed in a room on the right behind the altar; later he was revered as Saint Ina. Unusually, he had no obvious heir and according to Bede 'left his kingdom to younger men'.[36]

In one account of the *Brut y Tywysogion* (*Welsh Chronicles*), dated 683, Ivor, son of Alan, King of the Britons, having moved to Armorica (Brittany), invaded the south coast of England with a large army. He successfully fought off the Saxons who had taken over lands, reclaiming Somerset, Devon and Cornwall. Ivor, in thanks to God, gifted many lands to the church and built a monastery at Glastonbury. After maintaining the sovereignty for 39 years, he retired to Rome where he died.[34] This story is remarkably similar to King Ine's. Could Ivor the Briton be the Saxon King Ine? Geoffrey of Monmouth gives us a clue when he states that Ine was a nephew of Ivor and together they ruled over the last remaining Britons.[37] Whether he was British or Saxon, Ine succeeded in unifying the mixed races of southern Britain.

In 2006, I visited Rome to look for the tombs of the daughters of the British King Caractacus whose father was Bran. During my stay, I decided to visit the tomb of the great diplomat King Ine who shaped so much of the course of English history. The narrow streets of Vatican City were crowded with pilgrims and tourists making their way to St Peter's Square in the early afternoon heat. After a few inquiries, I arrived at the church of San Spirito in one of the side streets in Borgo. On entering through the main doors, I had to stop from going any further because a service was in full flow. I returned later that day to discover that prayers and services run perpetually throughout the day and the only opportunity to explore the building is just before it closes at 7 p.m.

After several refreshments at a side street café and another look around St Peter's Square with its eight-pointed star, I returned more determined than ever to see Ine's tomb. I entered just before 7 p.m., but the preacher was still

*San Spirito Church in Vatican City, Rome*

addressing the pilgrims in the bold Italian way, as if everybody was a sinner. Then within a minute of closing, he finished, so I walked swiftly to the front and entered the side chapel of Ine. I could just make out a shrine in the dim light over in the corner. My expectations rose as I approached the object of my quest, then suddenly there was darkness; I thought I had gone blind. As I stumbled back into the main church frustratingly tripping over the cushions, I saw that the priest had switched off the lights and was standing at the main doors. I tried to explain my quest to see the tomb, but he ignored my pleas, and before I could say Hail Mary, I was ushered out of the door. After experiencing the hype of the Vatican for longer than expected, I left the area with a feeling of disappointment and amusement at the day's events. I began to think that the universe was telling me that the spirit of Ine dwells not here in the back streets of the Vatican, but among the green fields of England and the rocks of Portland.

Although I had established that Ine held the manor of Portland as part of his inherited estates, I still questioned why he introduced 120 Jutes to settle on the island. I was able to unravel this mystery when I turned my attention to other areas of England settled by the Jutes.

The Venerable Bede (AD 672–735) was a monk and scholar who recorded English history that later served as a major source for *The Anglo-Saxon Chronicle*. He wrote:

> *"... the Jutes colonised the areas of Kent, Hampshire and the Isle of Wight, from the 5th century. They held these regions until 686, when the Saxon king, Caedwalla attacked them, killing their last and pagan king, Arwald, and captured his two younger brothers. These he forcibly converted to Christianity before executing them."*[36]

Ine's predecessor was King Caedwalla of Wessex (*c* AD 654–664). His malicious invasion of the Isle of Wight was an act of genocide; he murdered over 1000 Jutish families living on the island, particularly targeting the royalty amongst them.[38] Historians are puzzled as to why this massacre took place. Some believe Caedwalla wanted to expand his kingdom opposed by the 'heathen' Jutes. Bede states that during the invasion of the Isle of Wight Caedwalla was injured. This may account for his swift abdication and pilgrimage to Rome. On his arrival, he received baptism from Pope Sergius I on the Saturday before Easter and died 10 days later. His bones were laid to rest in St Peter's Church, now the Vatican – quite an honour for a former pagan king.

Did the Pope have contact with Caedwalla before his pilgrimage and order him to exterminate the Jutes because they opposed the new faith, or did the Isle of Wight Jutes possess teachings or knowledge that made them a threat to the Catholic religion? A similar fate befell the Cathars whose Gnostic religion was also in defiance of the Roman Catholic Church and the Pope who branded them heretics.

The effects of this Isle of Wight massacre succeeded in leaving present-day historians with little information about the origins of the Jutes; all that is known today is that they occupied large parts of what is now south Hampshire, Kent and the Isle of Wight and later merged with the Anglo-Saxons. One thing puzzled me though – why did Caedwalla specifically target the Isle of Wight Jutes over the others? What was so different about these people?

If it was the Pope's decision to exterminate the Jutes, then this order may have continued into the reign of King Ine. King Ine, having been related to these Jutes, made special provision for his surviving relatives from Kent and the Isle of Wight. Perhaps he secretly transferred them to his own manor of Portland, particularly those of royal descent, to ensure their safety on the fortress island.

# The Jutes

*The Anglo-Saxon Chronicle* shows that a few surviving Jutes were absorbed into the confederation of West Saxons, where they continued to form an important element of the Anglo-Saxon tribes. Osburgha, a young woman of royal Jutish blood and the daughter of Ealdorman Oslac of the Isle of Wight, a descendant of Whitgar, became Queen of the West Saxons (*c* AD 830). She married King Ethelwulf, a descendant of Cerdic, a Jute and first king of Wessex (as mentioned earlier), and had four sons. The youngest she named Alfred, who later became King Alfred the Great. Alfred ruled over Wessex and proudly claimed to be descended from the priestly Jutes.[39]

Cerdic was born in Jutland and reigned over Wessex between AD 519 and 534. He set sail with five ships from Jutland and arrived at Southampton Water in Hampshire in AD 495, where he and his nephews Whitgar and Stuf held their ground against the remaining British armies. Whitgar later ruled over the Isle of Wight and was buried at Carisbrooke Castle, once the site of a Saxon burgh or fort. Some historians believe Cerdic was partly British because of his name;[40] perhaps his mother was British.

Cerdic was descended from King Odin, a legendary figure from Scandinavian folklore. In the library of Heralds' College in London, a very ancient manuscript traces the lineage of the Danish kings, including Odin, right back to the biblical King David. Historians believe Odin was King Dan I whose reign over Scandinavia commenced in 1040 BC. The sagas reveal that his line stretched all the way back to the ancient Trojan kings.[41] The early British kings are traditionally descended from Brutus, a Trojan prince who landed in Britain around the same time and became the first (Trojan) king to rule this ancient land.[37]

The royal Jutish line of Wessex did not end with the invasion of the Normans. In about AD 1052 William the Conqueror married Matilda, a direct descendant of King Alfred the Great. Therefore, the tradition of the Whites of Portland having royal Jutish blood might well be correct, if they are indeed descendants of King Ine. I endeavoured to find further links between the Whites and the Jutes.

A most interesting book on Portland traditions is an out-of-print publication called *Old Portland. The Eighteenth and Nineteenth Century Memoirs of Elizabeth Pearce (later White) and Clara Jane White (later King Warry) of Portland Isle, Dorset*.[1] Both Elizabeth White and Clara Jane King Warry refer to the noble blood that runs through the veins of the Portland White family, to which King Warry belonged, and their close relationship to the Isle of Wight people as being of the same race.

I discovered further information that substantiates the surname White as having a definite link with the Jutes. The Anglo-Saxon *Winchester Chronicle* (AD 449) states:

> *"From the Jutes came the Cantware [inhabitants of Kent] and the Wihtware – that is the tribe which now lives in Wight – and that race in Wessex which they still call the race of the Jutes [Meonware]."[42]*

'Ware' is probably an Old English word for 'tribe', although in Welsh it means 'store' (as in 'warehouse'). The British called the Jutes of Kent the Cantware. The word 'Cant' derives from the Iron Age tribe Cantii which originally founded Canterbury before the Romans developed the town. The Cantware were a warrior race who helped the British King Vortigern fight off the Picts (ancient inhabitants of Scotland) after the Romans vacated Scotland. The Cantware built their capital at Canterbury over the Roman temples and built a Christian sanctuary there after their conversion, this becoming a holy centre for the later Anglo-Saxons and Normans.

The Meonware tribe of Jutes, also known as Ytes, settled in Hampshire in the Meon Valley opposite the Isle of Wight. After their conversion to Christianity they may have founded a religious centre at Winchester, which later became the religious capital of England. The name of the River Itchen that flows through the city is derived from its former Jutish name Ytene, and 'Meon' is an Old English word for 'middle' or 'holy'. This name, found only in Hampshire and Warwickshire, appears in ancient Israel at Beth Baal Meon, where the word translates to 'temple' or 'royal house'.

Historians write that the Jutish Wihtware or Whitwarra (tribe of Whit) who settled the Isle of Wight (a major Druidic centre) adopted the name of the island. However, just before the Saxon invasion the name of the island was Vectis, a Roman word for 'a place of division'. The island's name after the Jutes settled there is documented as Wit or Wiht.[43] Whit also occurs in the names of Jutish royals and religious leaders such as Wihtgils of Jutland, the father of Hengist, who came to Britain in AD 450. Whitgar the Jute was the nephew of Cerdic, the first king of Wessex. Wihtred (AD 690–692) was a Jutish King of Kent. Therefore, Whit is certainly a Jutish name.

During the time I was researching the name White, I took a weekend break to the Lizard peninsular in Cornwall. In a famous pasty shop, I noticed a clay figure of a witch with a long nose and pointed chin, a classic depiction seen in nursery books. I asked about the figure and the owner allowed me to examine it. Underneath, carved into the base, was the name St Win. Win is a Cornish name for White and means 'holy' or 'blessed'. In Cornwall, we find 'Win' in the place names of early centres of Christianity as well as in the names of some of the local saints, such as Winfrith, who is known to have Jutish origins. During his life, Winfrith visited Dorset and later the Isle of Wight where he became famous as St Boniface. Both Winchester, the British name, and Wihtchester, the Jutish name, have the same meaning – White or Holy City; even the later Normans made Winchester the spiritual centre of Britain.

The Dorset village of Whitchurch Canonicorum has been a place of pilgrimage for over a thousand years. The church there is dedicated to St Candida and the Holy Cross, and houses a lead box containing the bones of a small woman. Her name prior to the Middle Ages was St Wita or Wite, a virgin who lived the life of a hermit. Her well and shrine became a focus of pilgrimage for the healing of the sick up until the Reformation. Little is known of her origins; some local tales say she lived during the eighth century and was martyred during a Danish invasion. Was St Wita a descendant of the Jutish Whites of Portland?

Other instances of the name Whit or White are found in Jutish areas in the names of villages and land features, such as Whitwell and Whitcombe on the Isle of Wight and the villages of Whitechurch in Dorset and Hampshire. All these places have churches that date from the Saxon period and possibly before. The name Whit could also refer to light, shining or wisdom; Saxon kings always made decisions after consulting the Witan or Wiseman.[44] Whit Sunday, meaning 'Holy Day', dates from Saxon times. I believe Whit is a Jutish name for 'holy' or 'wise', and that the Whitwarra were the priesthood who taught religion to the other tribes.

According to the ancient *Welsh Triads*,[5] the Isle of Wight, Anglesey and the Isle of Man were long ago centres of religion, administered first by the Druid priesthood and later, after their conversion, by the Celtic Christian Culdees. It makes sense that if the Whitwarra were the priests of the Jutes they would aim to settle in one of Britain's religious centres on the south coast.

Apart from the ancient island custom of Gavelkind, finding further evidence of a Jutish settlement on Portland proved difficult. Maybe the place names can give us a clue: Ope is a Scandinavian term for 'sea shelters', such as Church Ope Cove and Longstone Ope. Nore, which also has Jutish connections, appears in God Nore Point and Blacknor Point. According to Susann Palmer:

> *"Virtually no definite archaeological remains of the Saxon period remain on Portland, but this is a problem found in other areas of England, even though there can be no doubt about it that the area was occupied by these invaders."*[12]

The only documented accounts concerning invasions of Portland are from a later date, AD 840, when Danes invaded the island and killed Aethelhelm,

Ealdorman of Dorset, and AD 982, when Danish pirates fought with the locals.[32]

## Jutish Artefacts

Excavations of Jutish settlements in Hampshire and on the Isle of Wight by the TV Time Team revealed artefacts of Gnostic and pagan nature, such as sixth century Byzantine 'situla' or buckets made from single sheets of brass and plated with tin. One of them, decorated with a beautiful frieze of leopards, mythical beasts and naked hunters, is inscribed "Use this lady for many happy years". The style of manufacture and the shape of the buckets with their decorations and inscriptions suggest that they came from the Eastern Byzantine Empire. The Time Team experts gave their best guess as Antioch in modern-day Syria, north of Israel; however, seafaring traders from fourth or fifth century Constantinople could have introduced them as souvenirs. Did the Jutes trade with the Middle East? The fact that there are no other Byzantine buckets found in England is a mystery. Perhaps buckets or cauldrons were ritual and ceremonial objects.

The Time Team discovered at both of the Jutish sites evidence of pagan practices, including temples, shrines, burials and cremations: "The varying status of burials indicates the different strata of a chiefdom society and the presence of grave goods is strong evidence for the early Jutes believing in the afterlife".[38] Recently Time Team researcher Barbara Yorke's evidence showed that there was a kingdom in Hampshire and the Isle of Wight from the fifth century onwards entirely populated by people whose ancestors lived in Jutland.

The Saxon historian Bede stated the Jutes' place of origin was Jutland, the earlier name for Denmark. Excavations of Jutish sites in Denmark reveal similar finds to those in Hampshire and on the Isle of Wight. A

*Byzantine bucket found at a Jutish site in Hampshire. (Permission of Hampshire County Museums Service/Winchester City Museum.)*

silver cauldron found in a Jutland bog in 1891 raised great excitement among archaeologists. Found near Gundestrup and dated to around 50–100 BC, it was at first thought to have been buried there as a ritual offering. Pollen analysis, however, proved that it was actually placed on dry earth that later became bog. This may indicate that Jutland was flooded after the burial of the object.

Although considered Celtic, the images depicted on the Gundestrup cauldron resemble those of south-eastern European, Greek, Iranian or Indian cultures rather than Celtic Irish or British. The depictions show divine beings and animals such as leopards and elephants, similar to the Hampshire bucket found by the Time Team. In fact, experts believe the cauldron depicts the history of Eastern influences spreading into Europe.[45] One of the images is that of a horned man bearing a remarkable resemblance to an Indus Valley seal. The ibises look Middle Eastern and the lions look decidedly Oriental. Scholars think it was a one-off find, part of some booty looted by Teutonic warriors, or even brought by migrating Celts from Thrace. However, I discovered after a little research that other cauldrons similar to the one found at Gundestrup have been unearthed in Denmark.

At this stage of the research the origin of the Whites of Portland is still a mystery, but we can establish that they came from what is today Denmark, and that they had some contact with southeast Europe or the Middle East. The Jutes migrated to Britain during a period of history called 'The Dark Ages', a time shrouded in myth and legend.

# Chapter 8

# A Dark Age of Catastrophe

When one culture successfully invades another, it seeks to boost its achievements by discrediting the history of the conquered race. The Roman, Saxon and Norman conquerors of Britain all succeeded in this mission. Those who seek to know the origins of our true British history will have a colossal task in unravelling fact from fantasy, although I believe, in the end, truth will always surface.

Archaeological evidence for the number of people living in Roman Britain before the arrival of the Jutes and Saxons now suggests that it was as high then as just before the Industrial Revolution in the nineteenth century – between 3 and 4 million. How a few thousand Saxons could change the culture and language of a country with such a large population in just a hundred years is a mystery.[1] Even today, the influx of over a million people into England from northern and eastern Europe has had little effect on our language and culture.

Hidden away and gathering dust is a wealth of information that suggests something cataclysmic took place after the Romans left, causing a huge decrease in the population and a vulnerability that I believe allowed the Jutes and Saxons to repopulate the country easily; remember, Bede, the monk historian, writes that they were invited in by the British Kings.

## Lost Lands and the Plague

Nigel Pennick drew on many legends and *The Anglo-Saxon Chronicle* in his book *Lost Cities and Sunken Lands* which reveals just how many places around the coast of Britain lost land to either floods or subsidence in the sixth century, as well as in 1099 as mentioned earlier (see 'Lost Lands' in Chapter 3).[2] After much research, I found evidence that refers to a geological disaster in England around AD 540, including tree ring data, ice core samples and documented history. Mike Baillie says "a climatic downturn became evident during this mysterious period when 'narrowest tree-ring' chronologies for AD 536 to 545 were observed".[3] Baillie cites the work of Dr Clube, who stated that fragments from the debris of a destroyed asteroid may have hit the Earth in the vicinity of northern Europe, causing plague, rising sea levels, tsunamis and tectonic plate movements in the sixth century.

Mysteriously, very few written documents survive from this tumultuous period of British history, but if you delve deep enough, there are still surviving accounts that reveal truly unbelievable events. Gildas, a British monk, recorded around AD 540 that the "island of Britain was on fire from sea to sea …. Until it had burned almost the whole surface of the island and was licking the western ocean with its fierce red tongue".[4] *The Life of St. Teilo*, part of the Welsh *Llandaf Charters*, records a plague witnessed by the Bishop:

> *"... however, he could not long remain [in Wales], on account of the pestilence which nearly destroyed the whole nation …. It was called the Yellow Pestilence, because it occasioned all persons who were seized by it to be yellow and without blood, and it appeared to men a column of a watery cloud, having one end trailing along the ground, and the other above, proceeding in the air, and passing through the whole country like a shower going through the bottom of valleys. Whatever living creatures it touched with its pestiferous blast, either immediately died, or sickened for death … and so greatly did the aforesaid destruction rage throughout the nation, that it caused the country to be nearly desert."[5]*

According to *The Life of St. Teilo*, St Teilo departed South Wales to escape the Yellow Plague, and stayed in Brittany for 11 years until it was safe to return.[5] *The Welsh Annals* also claim that between AD 537 and 550 there were plagues in Britain and Ireland, particularly in 547: "… a great death [plague] in which Maelgwn, King of Gwynedd died. Thus they say 'The long sleep of Maelgwn in the Court of Rhos'. Then was the Yellow plague".[6]

*The Anglo-Saxon Chronicle*[7] and *The Life of St Sampson of Dol*[8] record that towards the end of the fifth century and up to AD 550, Britons with enough wealth to support themselves emigrated across the Channel to the Armorique Peninsula. They named their new colony Bretagne (Brittany), and the Gauls called them 'Bretons'.[8] This made a lot of sense to me, as Brittany has many towns and churches named after sixth century Celtic British saints. These wealthy Britons from Cornwall, Wales and the southern counties fleeing the plague and migrating to the 'New Britain' (Brittany) left their former lands and possessions behind. Many of them never returned for fear of catching the plague or in the belief that the land was cursed. This allowed the northern Europeans to take over the vacated lands, settling peacefully during and after the plague.

Evidence shows that it was the Germanic or Danish aristocracy related to the British Kings who claimed the lands emptied by the Yellow Plague. As time went by these new settlers began to fight with local tribes, causing many British losses. Growing concern amongst the remaining British Kings eventually forced the reunification of the fragmented tribes led by Arthur, a brave warrior, who successfully fought off the newcomers in a series of legendary battles. Woven into the Arthurian myths were catastrophic events referring to Britain becoming 'the wastelands', when King Arthur and his famous knights set out on a quest for the Holy Grail in order to heal the sickened land.

For those with an interest in King Arthur, the Portland traditions actually refer to his local exploits. King Warry stated that the well-respected local historians Mr Freeman and Dr Guest believed Arthur fought his most famous victory against Cerdic in AD 520 at Badbury Rings.[9] Badbury Rings is another of Dorset's Iron Age fortified hills near the old town of Wimborne. Archaeological evidence also shows that Dorset was one of the last British frontiers against the Saxons during the Dark Ages. The ninth century British historian Nennius states that whilst Arthur fought his final battle at Camlann in AD 537, a plague ravaged Britain and Ireland.[6]

It is possible that the lack of documentary evidence from the Dark Ages was due to the censorship of records by Saxon monks after these catastrophic events. John Malalas, a sixth century Byzantine historian, recorded a substantial account of history up to AD 533 and after AD 540 but hardly anything in between, as if the records were purposely left out. Many historians believe the Anglo-Saxon monk historians, controlled by the papal power of Rome, deliberately suppressed the exploits of Arthur who supported British independence and the early Christian teachings. His fame was such that the British revered him as a god, and possibly a martyr, and therefore it is not beyond the realm of possibility that the Saxon historians may have edited and rewritten the history to suit their political agenda. Consequently, stories of Arthur and these natural disasters became mere myth and legend, including the sites of his battles and his burial place. The legacy of the Romans continued to haunt a divided southern Britain until a determined leader, King Ine, brought about an alliance of peace, setting the scene for the arrival of the Whit Jutes.

## The Bornholm Connection

The island of Bornholm off the coast of Denmark is barely 20 × 10 miles yet possesses 15 medieval churches and over a thousand megalithic standing stones. The location of some of the churches around the island indicates the geometric patterns of a pentagram and hexagram, similar to my findings on Portland. The Jutes also held this island as part of their territory. The architects of the Bornholm geometry appear to demonstrate the same skills in land surveying, geometry and mathematics as those on Portland. Authors Erling Haagensen and Henry Lincoln believed that medieval warrior monks called the Knights Templars may have built the churches, showing many extraordinary links between Bornholm, France and Jerusalem.[10]

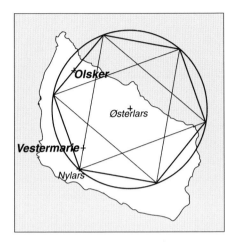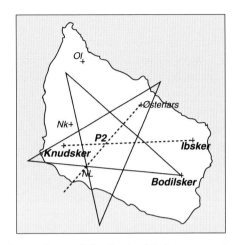

*The isle of Bornholm and its churches, with overlays of the Seal of Solomon and pentagram. P2 is the centre of the pentagram. O1, Olsker Church; Nk, Nyker Church; NL, Nylars Church. (From Haagensen, E. and Lincoln, H.,* The Templars' Secret Island: The Knights, the Priest and the Treasure *published by Weidenfeld and Nicolson, an imprint of The Orion Publishing Group, London.)*

Like Wales and many of the Scottish Western Isles, paganism existed alongside Christian worship on Bornholm up until the eleventh century, when it became a province of the Danes under King Knud (1035–1065). Knud was the English King Canute, whose royal estates included the Isle of Portland. Later, the growing power of Germany and the decline of royalty in Denmark allowed the Archbishopric of Hamburg in Germany to administer the country. Eventually, in 1104, the Pope, in a pact with Danish King Valdemar the Great, granted the people of Bornholm their own diocese. When Valdemar was a young boy he came under the guardianship of a noble and powerful Danish family called Hvide after his father was brutally murdered. Later, Valdemar, along with other members of this family, united Denmark.

A great change took place in the languages of northern Europe some time before 100 BC, whereby a great many words that had previously contained the sound of the letter D changed to the sound of T, and this is known as Grimm's Law.[11] L.A. Waddell writes:

> *"The interchange of the letters D to T is common throughout the whole family of Aryan languages, and is especially common even into the present day in Greece and amongst the Greek-speaking people of Asia Minor. Modern*

*guidebooks to Greece and Asia Minor warn travellers that the initial D of written or printed names is usually pronounced in the colloquial TH or T and the transposing of the O and R in the spelling is not infrequent. This change occurred during the years in which the Saxons were migrating to Western Europe from their presumed old home east of the Black Sea."[12]*

Moreover, in Danish Hv sounds like W. Thus Hvide translated into English becomes Wite or White.

Another member of this noble Danish White family was the very powerful Eskil, Archbishop of Lund. His close friendship with the founder of the Knights Templars, Bernard of Clairvaux of the aristocratic Burgundian family, may be significant. According to legend, it was prophesised at Bernard's birth that a great destiny lay before him. He became protector of the Knights Templars and, together with the Cistercian monks, helped finance their campaign in the Holy Land during the Crusades. Haagensen and Lincoln believe that the Knights Templars built the unique round churches of Bornholm, having built many similar churches around Europe and the Holy Land. The Templars may also have been responsible for sacred geometry in Jerusalem, as John Michell refers to the pattern of a pentagram found in the Holy City outlined by the way the streets meet inside the Damascus Gate at an angle of 36 degrees. At its centre is the rock of Golgotha, the supposed site of the Crucifixion.[13]

Although there is no evidence of the Knights Templars on Portland, King Warry refers to a quarry that once existed near the Verne prison called 'Hospital', a name that may be a reference to the Knights Hospitallers, an order that absorbed the Templars after their demise in 1313.[1]

# Chapter 9

# The Holy Land and Lost Tribes

The Jutes appear to have no recorded history of their race, and even their country of origin is subject to speculation by many modern historians. Nevertheless, some researchers are of the opinion that the Jutes were not exclusively from Jutland as Bede stated; the Frankish Rhineland and Frisia (Holland) may also be their place of origin. Evidence for this can be found in the early laws of Jutish Kent revealing a social system that is almost identical to that of the Frankish Rhineland and the Goth settlement of Frisia. Moreover, the field systems used by the Jutes of Kent resemble those of the area around the mouth of the Rhine, now part of present-day Germany.[1]

King Warry states that the Jutes who settled on Portland "had Goths amongst them"[2] and were more Frisian in their customs and place names. In earlier times, the Portland Jutes were tall and fair like the Dutch, but over centuries have become shorter and darker. Procopius, a fifth century Byzantine historian, wrote that the peoples of Frisia inhabited Britain in his day (*Goth*. Iv. 20).[3]

Although linguistic evidence seems to promote their place of origin as the Jutland peninsula, archaeological evidence suggests that Frisia and the area around the mouth of the Rhine were also Jutish settlements. This is most confusing and I was about to arrive at a dead end in the search for the true origins of the Jutes, when I unexpectedly came across an article about the use of language during the Saxon period. If Jute is the name given to this tribe by the English, then perhaps their continental name may differ. Grimm's Law, changing D to T, transforms Jute to Jude. A little more research revealed that in the Old English tongue of the Saxons, Jude is pronounced Yut, similar to the modern English word Jute.

Could Jude refer to the Jewish race or people from Judea in the southern part of historical Israel? The religion of the Jutes in Britain remained pagan right up until the seventh century. Apart from being polytheistic, the Jutes, like the Cathars, Goths and Merovingians, were Gnostic by their honouring of nature and the elements, whilst appearing to have no obvious parallels with the Jewish faith. Artefacts found in Jutish cemeteries also reveal no obvious connection with the Jewish culture.

The term Jew has become synonymous with the term Israel and Israelite, though many of today's historians believe this is misleading. Scriptural Israelites are not all Jews, unless associated by their religion Jew-dah-ism (Judaism); some of today's Jews may not be of the tribe of Yahudah (Judah) as many believe.[4]

Although there is no archaeological evidence that the Jutes had any cultural similarities to the Jews, there is a possibility that they took their name from their land of origin, namely Judea. Eventually I found a Danish tradition revealing the origins of the Jutes in a book called *The Tribes* written by Yair Davidiy, an expert on the ancient Israelites. He states:

> *"The Iatii (Yadi) in Europe were to become known as Jutes …. The Jutes were to settle in Denmark before participating in the invasion of England and a tradition from the Danish area related that the Jutes came from the Israelite Tribe of Judah and the Danes from Dan."*[5]

Author Walter Baucum also states his belief that the Jutes were part of the Biblical Lost Ten Tribes:

> *"A portion of the Tribe of Judah had been exiled with the other Ten Tribes. These particular Judaites among the northern Ten Tribes are recognizable in the Jutes, who were associated with the Dan peoples of Denmark."*[6]

Furthermore, he says that because so many Jutes or Yadi came to settle in Denmark, the country took the name of Judeland (Jutland), the land of the Judes. The archaeological finds in Denmark show that Celtic settlers, called by many authors Cimbri, arrived in Jutland around 300–250 BC. E. Raymond Capt, an expert in biblical archaeology, wrote:

> *"… one branch of the Cimmerians migrated from the Black Sea region in a north-western direction to the 'Low Countries' (now Belgium, Holland, and North-west Germany) to the 'German Ocean' and occupied the tract of land known as 'Cimbric Chersonesus' now called Jutland."*[7]

The Cimbri are also referred to by the Romans as the tribes that traded and settled around the Baltic and northern Europe. Plutarch states that they were originally known as the Cimmerians and thereafter as Cimbri, a race who were most probably ancestors of the Cimmerians.[8] Modern-day researchers also believe the Cymry or Cymri (Welsh) came from the Black Sea and may have links with the Lost Ten Tribes and be the ancestors of the Picts and Jutes. Historian Sharon Turner states that the word 'Cymry' is pronounced 'Kum-ree' or 'Kumri', which is identical to the name given to the captured Israelites by the

Assyrians.[9] Alan Millar says the word 'Cymry' is simply the Assyrian word for 'Israelites'.[10]

Both the Gundestrup cauldron found in Jutland, Denmark, and the Byzantine bucket found at a Jutish site in Hampshire had Eastern influences and one of the buckets probably came from Syria. Overall, the Jutish finds in England and Denmark are of a non-Christian nature and have links with cultures from the Black Sea area, where the Cimbri originated.

# Treasures in the British Museum

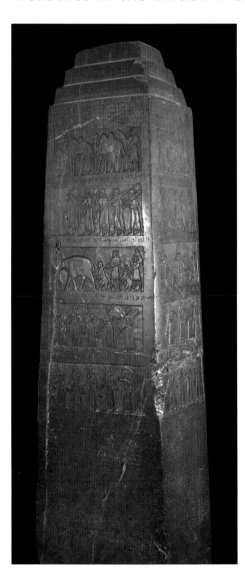

The British Museum in London houses a great collection of archaeological treasures from ancient Assyria. Recently one of its objects has given archaeologists and historical researchers an important clue to the identity of the Lost Tribes. I decided to view this object for myself, as it could also help my investigations into the mysterious Jutes. In the Ancient Near-East section of the museum, I found the Assyrian sculpture room. As a large crowd gathered around the gigantic winged human-headed lions that dominate the room, I noticed over the other side, amongst the statues of Assyrian Kings, the object of my quest, the Black Obelisk of Shalmaneser III.

In 1846, the archaeologist Henry Layard discovered the black limestone pillar during his excavations of the site of Ninevah (near Mosul in Iraq), the ancient Assyrian capital. The relief sculptures inscribed on the stone glorified King Shalmaneser III (858–824 BC) and

*The Black Obelisk. (© The Trustees of the British Museum. All rights reserved.)*

his chief minister. The second panel down from the top of the obelisk includes the earliest surviving picture of the Biblical Jehu, King of Israel, paying homage to the Assyrian Kings by bowing to the ground. Jehu was a direct descendant of Khumri (Omri), an earlier King of Samaria (Israel).[7] The Hebrew name Omri begins with the consonant 'y' and represents in Assyrian transliterations 'Kh'. The caption above the scene written in Assyrian cuneiform translates as follows:

> *"The tribute of Jehu, son of Khumri (Omri): I received from him silver, gold, a golden bowl, a golden vase with pointed bottom, golden tumblers, golden buckets, tin, a staff for a king and spear."*[7]

*Tribute of Jehu on the Black Obelisk. (© The Trustees of the British Museum. All rights reserved.)*

I wondered if the golden buckets, part of the tribute paid to the Assyrians, could be similar to those bronze buckets found by archaeologists on Jutish sites in Denmark and England.

In one of the rooms is a collection of Assyrian tablets that also relate to the conquest of 'Humria', better known as Israel, its peoples being the 'Khumri' or 'Kymry'; they also refer to Samaria in Israel as Bit Khumri. The Khumri (Israelites) eventually disappear from the Assyrian texts; many historians believe they integrated with the native Assyrians, becoming 'The Lost Tribes', although 'lost' only in terms of their identity and heritage rather than their physical disappearance.

Within the vast collection in the Assyrian rooms was another carving depicting the captured Israelites as slaves building cities and quarrying stone.

*Israelite slaves (above) and Assyrian slingers (below). (© The Trustees of the British Museum. All rights reserved.)*

Were these people ancestors of the Jutes whose relatives, the Whites, quarried Portland? Another panel shows Assyrian warriors slinging stones like 'the Ancients' who lived on Portland.

The amount of information I discovered about the Jutes and the Lost Tribes could fill a separate book. However, the connections I have found so far make some sense of why the papal-controlled Anglo-Saxon kings of southern Britain committed genocide on the Jutish peoples of England, yet spared the royals amongst them to strengthen their own bloodlines. Even though the Jutish descendants of the Royal House of David were a threat to the Pope and Catholic control of the western world, their bloodlines did continue through the female line of the Saxon kings. Even William the Conqueror chose to marry Matilda, a direct descendant of King Alfred the Great whose mother was a Jutish princess. This union of bloodlines brought forth a son, William II, also known as Rufus, the possible founder of the pentagonal Rufus Castle on Portland.

# Chapter 10

# The Trojan Britons

*"If the paralysing weight of convention and tradition is to be removed, it has long been apparent that the initial steps must be taken by someone who is free from the somewhat inordinate respect for the historians and their methods."[1]*

Many years ago, I came across an article in the Dorset County Museum written in the nineteenth century in *Somerset & Dorset, Notes & Queries*. I was surprised to read that the author considered Portland to be the landing place of Brutus, the legendary first king of Britain. He also believed that the cutting of the Cerne Giant commemorated the victory of Corinaeus over Gogmagog, and the name Cerne or Cernel derives from the Trojan general.[2]

Although sceptical of the link between Corinaeus and the Cerne Giant, I conceded that it was worth exploring further. I was indeed surprised to find legends and place names around Dorset associated with the fabled Trojan Britons. Realising the geographical importance of Portland, I considered whether they might have utilised the island sanctuary of Portland in the same manner as the Phoenicians, Romans and Saxons.

## Brutus and Portland

Archaeology reveals that the ancient Britons built and occupied many important sites in Dorset, including harbours such as Portland and strongholds such as Maiden Castle. Yet there is no mention of these important sites in the old Welsh records.

During the Saxon period, when the British tribes lost Dorset as part of their territories through either war or the Yellow Plague, the new immigrants renamed most of the towns and topographical features in their native Saxon language. The Britons, now confined to Wales and Cornwall, eventually forgot their former lands, transferring the names of their old historical places and heroes to their new settlements, hence the many Arthurian sites in Wales and Cornwall.

I became fascinated with the possibility that there might be a link between ancient Troy and Britain, especially as recent archaeological excavations in Turkey confirm that Troy did indeed exist. Until recently, historians and archaeologists did not take the story of Troy told by Homer in *The Iliad* seriously. Heinrich Schliemann (born 1822) was inspired by Homer's legends and, much to the disgust of the academics, used *The Iliad* as a guidebook. This controversial method paid dividends when he investigated the mounds at Hissarlik in north-west Turkey and discovered the great city. Over the following years, academics were still doubtful of the authenticity of the site, until a few years ago when they found the great outer walls, a discovery that erased any doubt. If the legend of Troy is true, then the old British legend that Brutus and the Trojans founded Britain could also be true.

According to old Welsh documents and many ancient legends recorded by both English and Continental writers, a Trojan prince called Brutus founded Britain and became its first king. Many literary sources referring to Brutus are available today, translated from accounts by the British monks Gildas in the fifth century, Tysilio in the seventh century, Nennius in the ninth century and Geoffrey of Monmouth in the twelfth century. Most relate to a story that began with Aeneas, a surviving member of the Trojan royal household, who fled from the destruction of Troy with his father Anchisis. They sailed west to escape the Greeks and landed in Italy upon the banks of the River Tiber, where a local ruler called Latinus welcomed them. Later Aeneas married Latinus's daughter Lavinia. Brutus was born as a result of the union between their grandson Silvius and their niece, who died giving birth to him.

A prophecy foretold that the boy would be to blame for the deaths of both his parents. At the age of 15 he accidentally killed his father with a bow and arrow while hunting. This event led to his banishment from Italy and forfeiture of his rights to the throne. Brutus made his way to Greece and settled with the Dorian Greeks. Here he met the descendants of Trojan slaves captured by the Greeks after the fall of Troy. They accepted Brutus as their leader and under his command raised an army against Pandrasus, the Dorian King. However, to avoid war, Pandrasus offered his daughter Ingnoge to Brutus in marriage instead, giving them ships to find new lands to settle.

They sailed west towards the Pillars of Hercules (Gibraltar) and landed on the island of Legrecia (believed by some to be Malta) to buy provisions. Although this island was deserted, Brutus found a ruined temple with an image of the goddess Diana. A myth describes how a certain form of ceremony, for those who consulted the Oracle, would allow the goddess to utter her responses. Brutus offered a sacrifice to the goddess, praying for guidance as to where to settle with his people. The prayer and answer, recounted in Latin by Gildas and reworked by the seventeenth century poet John Milton, goes as follows:

> *"Goddess of Shades, and Huntress, who at will*
> *Walk'st on the rolling sphere, and through the deep,*
> *On thy third reign, the earth, look now; and tell*
> *What land, what seat of rest, thou bid'st me seek;*
> *What certain seat, where I may worship thee,*
> *For aye, with temples vowed, and virgin quires."*

During his sleep by the altar, Brutus received this reply in a vision:

> *"Brutus, far to the west, in th' ocean wide,*
> *Beyond the realm of Gaul, a land there lies,*
> *Sea-girt it lies, where giants dwelt of old:*
> *Now void, it fits thy people. Thither bend*
> *Thy course: there shalt thou find a lasting seat;*
> *There to thy sons another Troy shall rise,*
> *And kings be born of thee, whose dreaded reign*
> *Shall awe the world, and conquer nation's bold."*[3]

Following directions given by the goddess Diana, they eventually, after many adventures, arrived at the shores of Britain in 1149 BC, then called Albion (the White Land). Brutus landed with a flotilla of 300 ships somewhere on the south coast at a strand named by Tysilio as Talnus, which Monmouth translated as Totness.[4] After exploring their promised land, Brutus and his followers encountered a marauding race of giants. After winning many subsequent battles, they successfully drove the remaining giants into the hills of Wales and Scotland, to the relief of the native inhabitants.

During the following celebrations, "… Brutus was proclaimed king, and at a national convention of the whole Island, with its dependences, was elected Sovereign Paramount".[5] A year later, during a festival and religious ceremony to commemorate their landing, the giants and their leader Gogmagog attacked, causing mass slaughter. Despite this, the Trojan Britons rallied, defeating the giants but sparing Gogmagog. Corinaeus, the mighty warrior general of Brutus's army (often depicted as a giant himself), demanded to wrestle with Gogmagog in a contest of strength in the true tradition of the Trojans.

During the competition, Gogmagog gripped Corinaeus and broke three of his ribs, enraging the general. After summoning all his strength, he heaved Gogmagog onto his shoulders and ran to the nearby coast, hurling him over the cliffs. The giant fell to his death landing on the sharp rocks below, staining them and the sea red. Monmouth cites Totness again as the location of the contest, although Tysilio says it took place next to the sea on a flat high rock above cliffs. However, Devon folklore claims Plymouth to be the historical place of the contest, as long ago a pair of giant figures wielding clubs was seen cut into the turf on the slope of the Hoe below the citadel. Elizabethan historian Richard Carew, who lived at Antony House on the opposite side of Plymouth Sound, wrote of the two figures:

> *"Moreover upon the Hawe at Plymouth, there is cut out in the ground the pourtrayture of two men, the one bigger, the one lesser, with clubbes in their hands (whom they term Gogmagog) and (as I have learned) it is renewed by order of the townsmen when cause requireth, which should infer the same to be a monument of some moment."*[6]

Brutus then went on to found a kingdom that was to incorporate the entire island of Britain and through his sons a great dynasty of kings emerged. This line of nobility eventually included the famous Caractacus, Boudicca and Cadwaller. Later, he constructed a city on the banks of the River Thames calling it Troia Nova or New Troy, which the Romans corrupted to Trinovantum. London legends recall how Brutus spared two of the giants, making them guardians of this new city.[5] Replicas of their statues stand in the Guildhall in the City of London.

The story of Brutus eventually became part of a pseudo-historical record of events known as 'The Matter of Britain', a name given by the twelfth century French poet Jean Bodel to distinguish Celtic traditions from the myths of classical antiquity. This account was widely accepted as historical fact up until the seventeenth and eighteenth centuries, when more reliable records and inscriptions became available.

A letter, well recorded by many historical researchers, adds validity to the Brutus legend. Before the invasion of Britain, Julius Caesar, standing on the opposite coast in Gaul, was curious about our island's history. His historians informed him that the peoples of this nation were of the same origin as the Romans, sharing the same ancestor – Aeneas. On hearing that long ago Brutus easily subdued Britain, Caesar thought that he too could quickly subjugate its inhabitants to the Senate of Rome. He sent a message to King Cassibellaun (Caswallon), son of King Lud, asking him to submit to Roman rule. Caswallon replied as follows:

> *"Cassibellaun, king of the Britons, to Caius Julius Caesar. We cannot but wonder, Caesar, at the avarice of the Roman people, since their insatiable thirst after money cannot let us alone whom the dangers of the ocean have placed in a manner out of the world; but they must have the presumption to covet our substance, which we have hitherto enjoyed in quiet. Neither is this indeed sufficient; we must also prefer subjection and slavery to them, before the enjoyment of our native liberty. Your demand therefore, Caesar,*

*is scandalous, since the same vein of nobility flows from Aeneas, in Britons and Romans, and one and the same chain of consanguinity shines in both: which ought to be a band of firm union and friendship. That was what you should have demanded of us, and not slavery: we have learned to admit of the one, but never to bear the other. And so much have we been accustomed to liberty, that we are perfectly ignorant what it is to submit to slavery. And if even the gods themselves should attempt to deprive us of our liberty, we would to the utmost of our power resist them in defence of it. Know then, Caesar, that we are ready to fight for that and our kingdom if, as you threaten, you shall attempt to invade Britain."*[7–9]

Monmouth claimed that the origins of the story of Brutus came from a Welsh source he called a "very ancient book". Although he omits to tell us its name and author, he does mention that Walter, Archdeacon of Oxford, obtained this book from Brittany. Geffrei Gaimar, an Anglo-Norman poet (*c* AD 1140), refers to the book as the "Good Book of Oxford". An early twentieth century archaeologist and historian Flinders Petrie believed he had identified the book as Tysilio's seventh century *Chronicle*, although he could not explain why it had received so little attention for centuries. Tysilio (AD 548–640) reportedly lived in Wales as a monk and rebuilt the monastery at Meifod, later founding a monastery at Suliac in Brittany where he wrote his *Chronicle of the Kings of Britain*.[10]

However, he records that Caedwalla died in 688, which took place after his own death in 640. This suggests that the monks at St Suliac may have continued his work. At the end of his book, a postscript by Walter of Oxford states "I, Walter, Archdeacon of Oxford, translated this book from the Welsh into Latin, and in my old age have again translated it from the Latin into Welsh".[10]

The book Monmouth used as his source may have originated in Brittany as at the time the country was a safe refuge for the British escaping the plagues, as mentioned earlier. Apart from the *Bible*, *The History of the Kings of Britain* by Monmouth succeeded in becoming the most influential history book in Britain during medieval times and even up to the Tudor period and is still in print today. However, he did have his critics. In AD 1190 a Norman historian, William of Newburgh, suggested that Monmouth, born a Welshman, invented most of the history "From an inordinate love of lying or for the sake of pleasing the Britons".[8]

Robert, Earl of Gloucester and Glamorgan had a hand in Monmouth's book for he was its principal dedicatee. He was the illegitimate son of King Henry I and Nest, the daughter of Iestyn, King of Glamorgan. As a direct descendant of Brutus through the line of the Glamorgan kings, he believed that Monmouth's book would award him greater popularity with the mistrustful English who already despised the Norman barons, furthering his claim to the throne. Unfortunately, the Pope declined to recognise him as a member of the Royal

House, so his only option was to side with Matilda in her war to claim the throne from Stephen after the death of Henry I. During this conflict, Robert captured Rufus Castle on Portland in 1142 on Matilda's behalf. Bettey claims that the Castle took its name from Robert of Gloucester, as he was also known as Rufus, a nickname meaning 'red haired'.[11]

Not surprisingly *The History of the Kings of Britain* finally fell from grace during the reign of Henry VIII when the Roman Catholic priest Polydore Vergil (*c* 1470–1555) published his *Anglica Historia* in 1534 denouncing the entire history of the Britons with the following words:

> *"Trulie ther is nothinge more obscure, more uncertaine, or unknowne then the affaires of the Brittons from the beginninge."[12]*

The events that followed the publication of this book were inexplicable; after 300 years of being unchallenged, the whole history of the Britons fell from favour and Welsh sources were discarded, including those of Nennius and Gildas.

## The Brutus Stone

Brutus and his bloodline continued to intrigue me, and in amongst the myths and legends and early written accounts I felt sure I would find a link with Portland.

Monmouth cites Totnes in Devon as the landing place of the Trojan fleet. The town lies a few miles inland from Dartmouth on the River Dart. In the High Street (Fore St.) is a granite stone set into the pavement with a sign pointing to the Brutus Stone. Local lore states that the stone marks the place where Brutus first set foot on land, uttering as he did so: "Here I stand and here I rest, And this town shall be called Totnes".[12a]

*The Brutus Stone, Totnes, Devon.*

In Totnes library I discovered that the stone is a natural granite boulder probably deposited during the Ice Age. It may have been used as a landmark along a track near the ancient fording of the River Dart. In 1810, the stone was broken up and levelled flat with the pavement to allow for the widening of the street. I could find no mention of an actual stone called 'The Brutus Stone' in any of the town's old records, although in 1473 a 'Broadstone' once stood outside the west gate marking the course of the water from Harpers Spring.[12]

Another local tradition says that the Mayor would stand upon the Brutus Stone to announce the accession of a new monarch and even the Town Crier hailed the news of the day from there. However, from at least 1459 'Brutt' was a medieval Devonian word for news given by a town crier, making the stone a more likely candidate for a 'Bruiters Stone'. Therefore, I concluded that Monmouth mistranslated Talnus, the landing place of Brutus, to Totnes.[6]

Moreover, Monmouth's version of the contest between Corinaeus and Gogmagog states that the Trojan general ran with the giant on his shoulders from Totnes, the port of landing, to nearby cliffs and threw him over. This is very unlikely as local maps show the nearest cliffs from Totnes are 9 miles away. Later versions of the story depart from the original by placing the contest at Plymouth, perhaps because of the figures carved into the hillside of the Hoe, recalled by Richard Carew.

The Welsh documents translated by Monmouth also describe Totnes as a port, but evidence from local archaeology provides proof that the town did not exist as a port when Brutus arrived around 1149 BC; in fact no settlement existed there until the late Saxon period.[12] Furthermore, archaeological finds prove that Totnes was not a recognised port until the Norman period and also there are no local folktales of giants, except for the Brutus story. Visiting the mouth of the River Dart, I noticed something else; the river would have been too narrow and too vulnerable to attack from the hills flanking either side for the safe passage of 300 Trojan ships on their way to Totnes. It seems unlikely that Brutus would risk his fleet by sailing through such a place. This all made me conclude that if the story of Brutus was true then Totnes could not be his place of landing.

The archaeology of Portland does suggest that a port existed here for many centuries, including the period when Brutus supposedly landed in Britain, and most importantly that it was large enough to accommodate a fleet of 300 ships. In ancient times, mariners, upon arrival, would celebrate their safe journey by honouring the gods or goddesses at unhewn stone altars. Having discovered that the Brutus Stone in Totnes was a place of declaration and not a holy stone or altar, I then came to the conclusion that it was woven into the folklore of Brutus upon publication of Monmouth's book.[6]

There were many accounts of stones and altars existing on Portland before the interior quarrying. In the nineteenth century, a field near the Avalanche Church in Southwell had the name Brutt Stone Meadow, named after a 'Brutt' stone, now destroyed.[13] This forgotten stone could be the famous altar erected by Brutus or 'Brut', as early documents often called him. In the surrounding area where the Brutt stone once stood, many artefacts from the period of Brutus have been unearthed. One of the Portland field names mentioned earlier is Parrates Acre, or Barrates Acre; this may be another indication that Brut and the early Britons visited this island. According to L.A. Waddell, Barats or Barati were the royal elite of the Aryans, including the Trojans who became known as Barat-ana ('ana' meaning 'one'), one of the Barats (Bruits) or Britons.[14]

In 1723, Tristram Risdon wrote that when Brutus arrived at a port on the coast of Britain, "He called this place Tout al esse … and in tract of time, without any great alteration, hath been changed into Tout a ness, now contractedly Totnes".[15] William Bowles noted in 1828 that "most of the hills of the sea coast, and through Dorsetshire, are still pronounced Teuts (Toots) by the common people".[16] As we know, Portlanders lived in relative isolation from the mainland, resulting in many of the old British place names surviving on the island, one of which is Tout (Tot), a word meaning 'lookout'. The name occurs in different parts of Portland, such as Tout Quarry above Chesil, Toutfield near Rufus Castle, Long Tout near the Grove, North Tout Weir in the East Weares and South Tout near Southwell. The strategic situation of Portland is ideal as a lookout or 'tout' for any possible invasions along the Wessex coast. Could Tout be one of the early British names for Portland? Although Monmouth would have known that Portland was a Royal Manor of the Norman Kings, he may not have been aware of any earlier British names for the island.

Alternatively, Roberts, who translated Tysilio's *The Chronicle of the British Kings of Britain*, refers to Talnus, the place of Brutus's landing, as a raised tumulus: "If this word be correctly given, it may be considered as a Phoenician name, derived from Tel nesua, i.e. tumulus elevatus".[10] Perhaps this is a clue to the location of the true landing place of the Trojans, as sailing along the south coast of Britain from the east, Portland looks like a tumulus raised from the sea. In an effort to find a plausible match for Talnus, perhaps Monmouth may have simply assumed Totnes as being the likely choice, without looking into any further possibilities.

Tysilio also describes the site of contest between Corinaeus and Gogmagog as taking place by the seaside on a flat high rock above cliffs. The high plateau and cliffs of Portland fit this description perfectly. In Celtic and Saxon lore, places of contest, either legal or trial by combat, were held on islands with causeways such as Portland. The Celts believed the causeway was a connecting passage symbolising an umbilical cord linking the realms of the living on the mainland with the mystical realms of the dead. This allowed access for mortals to honour the gods and their buried kings at sacred times of the solar and lunar year. On the Isle of Alney in the Thames, tradition says a fateful duel took place in AD 1016 between King Canute and Edmund Ironside to decide who would be King of England.[17]

One other peculiarity that may support Portland as an early place of kingship is the fact that the ancient coat of arms of Melcombe Regis, opposite Portland, has the three royal lions.

# The Giants of Old

The place of contest between Gogmagog and Corinaeus may have been the high flat rock once the centre of the island upon which Rufus Castle now stands. The earlier name for Rufus Castle was Giant's Castle, referred to in the former name of the old Alessandra Hotel in nearby Wakeham.[18] Dorset and Portland folklore has many references to giants, whereas South Devon has very few. These traditions may have derived from the shorter Celtic Iron Age peoples who, like the Trojans, arrived from the Mediterranean and encountered the taller blonde Nordic natives, descendants of the Bronze Age culture of Wessex. The old Portland traditions speak of 'mighty men of old', a race of stone-slinging giants who lived in the Verne hillfort. Dorset folklore also claims that giants built the hillforts of Maiden Castle (the largest and most impressive hillfort in Europe), Badbury Rings and Spetisbury Rings.[19]

The ancient figure of a naked giant warrior wielding a club resides 17 miles north of Portland, cut into the hillside above Cerne Abbas. Cerne is an ancient British word supposedly taken from the name of the river that runs through the village. However, Peter Roberts states that 'Corinaeus' in the Welsh language is 'Ceryn'.[10] Perhaps the giant is a depiction of Corinaeus, his name later corrupted to Cerne, cut as a memorial to his famous battle on Portland. Maybe the giant marks his burial place, his bones resting nearby. Mysterious Iron Age mounds and earthworks surround the hill figure, possibly the remains of an important prehistoric tribal meeting or religious centre.[18a]

On Portland, a seventeenth century story tells of a large earthquake that caused cracks to open up near the Verne where quarry workers saw giant skeletons within the fissures but failed to recover them. Quarry workers in the nineteenth century also called the mysterious corbelled underground chambers they found in many of the quarries 'giant's beehives'. Another Portland tale refers to the discovery of giants' coffins near the Grove, some measuring 10 ft in length. Most were destroyed, apart from a few smaller coffins now in the local museum.[18]

A skeleton 7 ft tall, unearthed at Flowers Barrow near Lulworth Cove in Dorset, had its decapitated head facing west, a different orientation to the rest of the skeleton.[20] This story is reminiscent of Bran, whose head was removed to protect Britain (see Chapter 2). British and Irish myths refer to Bran as one of the beneficent giants and so large that no house could contain him.[21]

The old Portlanders were renowned for their large stature, and it is possible that these tales allude to ancient memories of a race of tall people who settled there long ago. Around the British Isles, there are many legends and traditions of an ancient race of giants. Most people believe 'the mighty men of old' are a myth originating in folk tales and nursery rhymes, as no concrete evidence exists, despite the fact that many stories and legends of giants are found in different countries around the world. They are particularly prevalent in the Eddas of the Norse, in the legends of Persia and India and in the tales of the Greenlanders. Even the world's holiest books such as the *Bible* and *Koran* and some of the earliest historical manuscripts refer to them.

There are reports of finding giant human bones around the world, but they seem to crumble to dust with exposure to air, or later mysteriously disappear. One remarkable incident, mentioned in the memoirs of St Patrick, records the discovery of a large skeleton found while he was supervising the excavation of an ancient mound in Ireland. This giant was over 12 ft in length, wearing rusting armour, and alongside him lay an almost decomposed axe and a long sword. Patrick, in awe of the size and age of this once great warrior, promptly ordered its permanent dispersal, including the weaponry.[22] (St Patrick deliberately destroyed many of the old pagan traditions in Ireland, including potential idols like the giant warrior.)

*The Book of Enoch* recalls the history of a race of giants originating in the Middle East. According to the book, the great god Anu sent a flood to destroy this "wicked race", with any survivors hunted to extinction. Sumerian and Hittite seals depict the priests and royalty nearly twice the size of ordinary humans, but scholars believe these depictions are merely a statement of their power over their subjects.

In the *Bible*, Moses sent spies to seek out fertile land in the region of Kadesh. Reports came back that a race of giant men occupied the land:[23]

> *"... And there we saw the Nephilim, the sons of Anak, who come of the Nephilim; and we seemed to ourselves like grasshoppers, and so we seemed to them." (Numbers 13:33)*

The *Bible* also states that God told Joshua to enter the land of Canaan and destroy the Amorite Giants, whose leader was Og. He succeeded in driving them into the northern regions of Israel to a narrow strip on the Syrian coast, which later became the home of the Canaanite-Phoenicians.

Near the ancient prehistoric centre of Avebury are the villages of Ogbourne St Andrew and Ogbourne St George, both villages having a great mound, known as 'Giant's Grave'. Other examples are Ogbury near Stonehenge and Ogmore valley in South Wales. Oghma was the Irish god of literature and eloquence. He was the son of De Dagda and the champion of the Tuatha de Dannan. He invented the Ogham script, from which the later Druidic alphabet derives. Even our folk and fairy tales refer to giant monsters as Ogres.

The contest between Gogmagog or Goemagot (the early version of the name) and Corinaeus seems to fit the geography and place names of Portland and supports my belief that it was the isle of contest rather than Totnes or Plymouth. Close to Portland Pike, the place where legend says the devil or giant threw great boulders across to Portesham Down, is Maggot Quarry. This ancient name originates from a field that existed here before quarrying.[13] Fido Lunettes, on a visit to Maggot Quarry around 1825, saw the remains of what may have been a prehistoric cromlech, perhaps the grave of the giant Goemagot killed by Corinaeus. Lunettes also visited an ancient British earthwork, now destroyed, near the Grove called Arun's Green. A local tradition says a great battle took place here; could this be the site of the great contest?

Dorset has many pairs of ancient trees named after the fallen Gogmagog, whereas Devon has none. Only a few miles from the hill figure of the Cerne Giant are two pairs of ancient trees called Gog and Magog; a pair of oaks near Glanvilles Wootton and a pair of beeches near the eminence of High Stoy share the same name.[18]

The hillforts of southern Britain belong to the period of Celtic migrations from Europe. In the Middle East, we find their equivalent in the fortified towns and cities of Israel. The walls of Troy were labyrinthine in a similar fashion to Dorset's Maiden Castle. To the east of Maiden Castle is a small hamlet beneath a prominent hill with the name of Troy Town, referring to an earth-cut labyrinth that once existed on the hill overlooking Dorchester and Maiden Castle. Other Troy Towns or Miz Mazes in Dorset existed near Bere Regis, Blandford and Leigh.[24] The ancient practice of making and walking the labyrinth continued here in Dorset more than in any other county in Britain, possibly originating from the Trojan immigrants.

To the west of Portland, the next natural harbour is West Bay close to the old town of Bridport. Many believe the name Bridport derives from the River Bride which flows out to sea a couple of miles to the east; others say that the Brit River, which meanders through the town, lent its name to Bridport. Historical research proves both these ideas to be false, as the original name for the Brit River was the Woosh; it was renamed Brit in more recent times. Hutchins, a sixteenth century antiquarian, wrote that the original name for Bridport was Bruteport, supposedly named after a visit by the legendary Trojan leader.[19] Again, the interchange of the 'd' and 't' in northern European languages, referred to earlier, turns the original name of Brit into Brid.

Hutchins also wrote that Dorchester takes its name from Dorn, a local British king who was a descendant of Trojan "Brutus and the fabulous founders of the British Cities".[19] Dorn is said to have built the town and resided in his palace at Maiden Castle. Dorn was probably responsible for building the labyrinth of earthen walls at Maiden Castle based on the traditions of ancient Troy. At the meeting place of a number of ancient trading routes, Maiden Castle may have had another purpose during its history, as archaeologists believe the sheer size and circumference of the hillfort would require several thousand men to defend its walls. However, the east and west entrances connected by a cursus, or raised earthen causeway, may have been more for ceremonial purposes. Artefacts found here were also of a religious nature. The later Romano-British temple built within the fort may signify the continuation of ceremonial use at this site.

The finding of gold in some of the Bronze Age mounds around Dorchester during Victorian times triggered a form of greed, not unlike the Klondike gold rush in America. This resulted in a great loss of ancient artefacts as well as severe damage to the ancient mounds. The gold may have originally journeyed to Portland from the ancient mines in Ireland via Dorchester along a recognised prehistoric overland route from Porlock on the north coast of Somerset.[25] The Britons would have regarded this route as the safest journey for their valuable cargo rather than risk the perilous sea journey around Cornwall.

It is unfortunate that archaeology has become divorced from folklore, as neither two subjects can advance significantly without the aid of the other. For me, science has stripped away the romance and mystery that once surrounded the archaeological scene. Yet archaelogist Heinrich Schliemann embraced the romance of ancient myths and legends, leading him to one of the greatest finds in the history of archaeology with the discovery of Troy.

## Traditions of the British Race

From Elizabethan days up until the reign of King George I, our British history books told a story most people would regard as fable today, and they may be correct, as some of these stories may be exaggerations and contain untruths; but alas, they are no longer available for our scrutiny. Long ago, by the light of a fire, people all over the country recounted oral traditions of the British race, just as the old Portlanders did. Unfortunately, during the last hundred years or so these legends were discouraged, until they disappeared almost completely from our sphere of history. When Henry VII, son of Edmund Tudor, won the battle of Bosworth the bloodline of the ancient British kings or Trojans returned to the throne of England once more. His son Arthur, Prince of Wales, was next in line to become King Arthur II, with his bride Catherine of Aragon as queen. However, he died before this happened and the throne and his wife passed to his brother Henry, who became Henry VIII. During his reign, England became divorced from the power of Rome for the first time since the Roman invasion, heralding the start of a new freedom for historians who, until then, had to conform to papal laws. Our ancient British history returned once again to the public domain thanks to Raphael Holinshed, who collected manuscripts and Bardic traditions from around the country to compile the *Chronicles of England, Scotland and Ireland* (AD 1577). These include the following British creation myths:

*"The flood reduced the earth's population to Noah's three sons Shem, Ham and Japheth. They re-peopled the Earth by starting new tribes in each continent, the Middle East by Shem (Semites) Africa by Ham (the Hamatic race) and Europe by Japheth."*[26]

The *Chronicles* continue to describe how Japheth's son Samothes introduced a colony to Britain 200 years after the Flood, naming the island Samothea. His successors were Magus, Sarronius, Druiyus, Bardus, Longho, Bardus II, Lucus and Celtes. Albion, allegedly one of the giant sons of the god Neptune, defeated Celtes and subdued the island, renaming it Albion. His reign lasted until Hercules slew him.[26] Perhaps the giant on the hill above Cerne Abbas, said to represent Hercules, was cut by locals inspired by this ancient folk tradition. Britain continued to be called Albion, ruled over by a succession of kings, until Brutus the Trojan Prince arrived in 1149 BC and named the island Britain (see Appendix B).

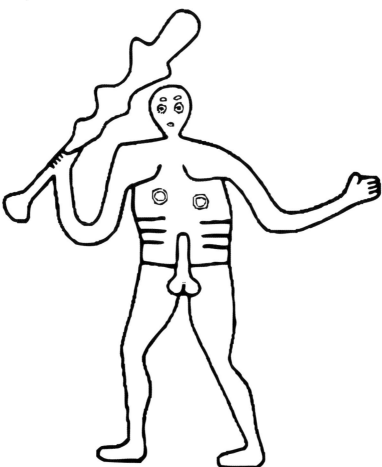

*Could the Cerne Giant be a memorial to Corinaeus?*

# Chapter 11

# The Discovery of a Landscape Figure

*"Traditional teachings inform us that the earth is not a dead body, but is infused by a spirit that is its life and soul. It is a world where the material is a reflection of the spirit, and where the spirit reveals itself in the material."*[1]

Having completed the research on giants and their connection with Portland, I noticed the outline of a colossal human figure shaped from the field boundaries, footpaths and roads on a satellite photograph of the island. The seemingly giant male figure has both arms held above his head in the classic posture of invocation, found in many early depictions of gods and goddesses in the act of summoning spirits. The figure also reminded me of Corinaeus the Trojan who threw Goemagot over the cliffs. In fact, the giant appears as though he is in the act of throwing something over the cliffs and at the very location where Lunettes describes a British earthwork called Arun's Green, the site of a great battle north of the Grove.

Three of Portland's great fields and their ancient boundaries make up the main portion of his giant body. Inmosthay Field between Wide Street and Easton Lane forms his upper arm, Droop Field between Easton and Weston his upper torso, and Coombe Field between Weston and Southwell his lower torso. The road to the Grove from Easton Lane forms the outline of the back of his head, and the road to the Bill from Southwell outlines one of his legs.

I also discovered that the ancient sites and places of importance on Portland, which we have visited throughout this book, play a vital role in the makeup of this landscape figure.

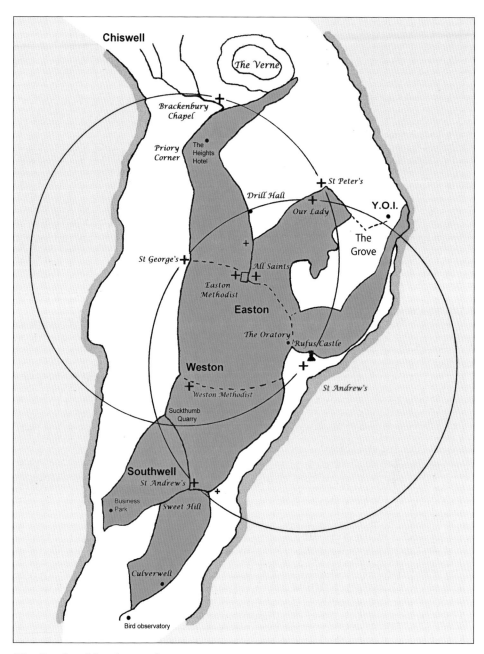

*The Portland landscape figure.*

# The Portland Giant

- With St Peter's Church at his crown, he faces east where ancient priests honoured the rising sun and moon.
- One hand holds the weight of the Verne prison, the site of the old hillfort, above his head, while the other supports the Young Offenders Institution, once the site of the Druid Grove.
- The churches at the centre of the circles, St Andrew's and St George's, are under each arm as if to support him.
- His torso is formed from the roads leading from these churches to St Andrew's Avalanche Church at Southwell, positioned at his groin.
- The road to Culverwell, with two paths from Sweet Hill and Suckthumb Quarry, form his mighty legs. The small cross is an old Methodist Chapel, now a private house in Southwell Street.
- His heart is at the centre of the Vesica, which contains the All-Seeing Eye, with the upper and lower points of the Vesica balanced on the right hip and the crown of his head.
- The fusion of the Vesica Piscis with the giant creates a marriage of male and female.

If we combine the folklore and history with the design there is some interesting symbolism:

- The giant holds the ancient fortress of the Verne like a stone in his right hand, a place where tall slingers fought contests and defended their island.
- Between his left hand and his temple lies the sacred precinct of the Druids and the megalithic priesthood.
- He leans forward against the sacred 'High Place' or Giant's Castle (Rufus Castle), under his arm.
- In the centre of his neck is All Saints' Church, Easton, the 'Mark Point' of King Warry.
- At the groin is St Andrew's Avalanche Church and site of the well and spring at Southwell.
- His knee rests on the ancient settlement and spring at Culverwell.

Many giant landscape figures have been found throughout Britain, formed from natural features and man-made paths and roads, whose shapes defy explanation. With the advent of aerial photography, many of these landscape figures have become more apparent. *A Guide to Glastonbury's Temple of the Stars* by Katherine Maltwood illustrates a complex pattern of giant figures, both human and animal, forming a circular chart of the zodiac, 10 miles in diameter and made from the contours and landmarks around Glastonbury in Somerset.

Each of the figures corresponds with their respective stars: for example, the stars of Virgo fall within the giant figure of the goddess, the stars of Leo fall within the lion figure, and so on. The calculated odds for this happening by chance are millions to one.[2]

A few years ago, inspired by Maltwood's book, I set off to explore other reported examples, including the giant figures of the Priscelli Zodiac in Wales[3] and the Lizard Zodiac in Cornwall,[4] and came to a puzzling conclusion. Many of the figures have within their design man-made footpaths and roads built fairly recently, with inexplicable turns and twists that make no sense on the ground but fit the overall design from above, as if the hand of man was unconsciously guided by the spirit of the place.

Those who have a deep affinity with the natural environment often sense the spirit of a place, called a 'Genius Loci'. In Etruscan mythology, this was the protective intelligence or elemental essence of the local landscape, often depicted as a serpent. On an unconscious level, the Genius Loci may be the creative force that provides the inspiration for sensitive people such as psychics, artists and poets. The Spirit may also guide them to worship or create a local god or goddess as a physical representation in the landscape, such as a rock carving.

Portland has so many layers of hidden symbolism that permeate the island. Like several of the terrestrial figures around the country, the Portland giant has evolved from the forming of paths over a long period, guided by the hand of man as he unconsciously tuned into the Genius Loci. As mentioned in the Introduction, the Celts, who revered the islands that surround Britain, gave to each of them a specific deity or spirit of protection, honouring them at solar and lunar festivals throughout the year. Could this giant male figure represent 'the Spirit of Portland', and, if so, who is he?

The visionary artist William Blake (1757–1827) personified Albion as a giant, associating him with Cronos. According to the Greek biographer Plutarch (AD 46–127), Cronos lies sleeping beneath an island of Britain, fettered by chains and guarded by deities. Plutarch recording the legend states:

> "... moreover there is, they say, an island in which Cronos is imprisoned, with Briaeus (a giant) keeping guard over him as he sleeps; for, as they put it, sleep is the bond forged for Cronos, and that around him are many divinities, his henchmen and attendants."[5]

Plutarch mentions Briaeus, a giant who keeps guard over him. Could this be the Portland giant? The myth referred to by Plutarch has some parallels with the age-old legend of King Arthur and the immortal gods of Irish and Welsh folklore, who also sleep beneath an island off the coast of Britain. Tacitus, the Roman historian, mentions that Cronos, also known as 'Father Time', was the ruler and god of the 'Golden Age' in Greece until his son Zeus deposed him and banished him as a prisoner to Britain.[6]

Could this tradition concerning a legendary god king of ancient Greece in Britain be an allegory? If we look at local archaeology, there are finds that indicate a lively trade with Greece during the Bronze Age. It is possible that a colony, probably Phoenician, emigrated from Greece during the decline of their empire to continue their so-called Golden Age here on the outermost islands of Europe, safe from conflict. Perhaps one of the great barrows on Portland, such as King Barrow, is a grave of a Phoenician or Greek king.

The British tales of Cronos differ slightly from that of the Greek, and I began to notice that the Cronos legend parallels that of Bran who rules over a similar otherworldly realm. Robert Graves refers to the name Cronos in his book *The White Goddess* and states:

> *"For though the later Greeks liked to think that the name meant chronos, 'time,' because any very old man was humorously called 'Cronos,' the more likely derivation is from the same root cron or corn that gives the Greek and Latin words for crow–corone [or korone] and cornix. The crow was a bird much consulted by augurs and symbolic, in Italy as in Greece, of long life. Thus it is possible that another name for Cronos [Kronos] ... was Bran, the Crow-god."[7]*

Many gods and kings of the ancient world are associated with the cult of the Crow or Raven, including Cronus, Bran, Arthur, Apollo, Odin and Lugh. Graves also mentions that Roman statues of Cronos and Saturn have him armed with a crooked dagger or pruning knife that resembles a crow's bill. Perhaps the early settlers of Portland noticed that the unusual crooked shape of the island is like the bill of a crow, which the Romans attributed to their god Saturn, and which the British Celts attributed to Bran.

Bran is a common name on Portland, with a prehistoric burial mound and a valley and a hill thus named. According to the old British tales, Bran is a giant. Perhaps the giant landscape male figure represents Bran, and therefore Bran is the Genius Loci, the Spirit of Portland.

# A String of Magical Islands

In the Introduction, I mentioned that the Celts and Druids viewed the islands that surround Britain as sacred, particularly Iona, Anglesey and the Isle of Man. In Chapter 6, I showed how many of Portland's churches lie on accurate straight lines called leys. Imagine my surprise when I discovered that a ley projected from Portland links these sacred isles together.

Since the 1970s, long-distant alignments have been discovered and researched, such as the St Michael Line from Land's End to the Norfolk coast[8] and the Apollo alignment through Europe from Skellig Michael in Ireland to the Apollo sanctuaries of Delphi and Delos in Greece.[9] The study of these long-distance leys reveals that ancient man was able to survey vast distances, linking sacred sites together with incredible accuracy. My own investigation of the 'Belinus Line', which connects many important prehistoric sites and historical cities, from the Isle of Wight to Durness on the north coast of Scotland, also contributes to this research.[10]

The possibility that Portland lies upon such an alignment fascinated me, but it was not until I had completed the very last section of this book that I made the discovery. A friend of mine who is a qualified dowser and geomancer confronted me with his discovery that Portland connects with other sacred islands on a ley from the Callanish stone circle in Scotland, through Whithorn and the Isle of Man. During my own investigations of this line and a little experimentation using large detailed maps, I discovered another remarkable string of magical islands that connects Iona with Portland.

A line drawn from Rufus Castle on Portland to Iona passes through the Isle of Man and Anglesey, linking the most revered isles of the Druids and the Celts. Could this be just a coincidence? Checking this ley for accuracy with computer programs and detailed maps dispelled any doubts that the curvature of the earth will have an effect on the alignment.

The line continues north after Iona to another sacred isle between North and South Uist called Benbecular. Not so long ago this isle was accessible only by fording at low tide along causeways marked by cairns between North and South Uist. Near its main town of Balivanich, Gaelic for 'town of the monks', the alignment passes through the remains of a sixth century church called Teampull Chaluimchille (Columba's Temple). The Benedictine monks who ruled over Portland also had a monastery on this island. Benbecular is also famous for the capture and burial of a mermaid, similar to the tale told on Portland.[11]

The isle of Iona is only 3 miles long and 1.5 miles wide yet it stands out in comparison to many of the world's sacred sites. Historians believe its sanctity is due to the reverence given to the isle by early Celtic Christians such as St Columba, and the mystical order of the Druids, who set up a college there for education in their religion, naming the isle Druidhneach or 'Isle of the Druids'. From the seventh to the eleventh century, many Scottish, Irish and Norwegian kings, warriors and martyrs rest here in the sanctified soil outside Iona's Cathedral.[12]

Why a remote tiny island off the coast of the Isle of Mull in the Western Isles of Scotland became so holy is a mystery. Perhaps its secret, like Portland's, lies within its unique geology. Thrust up in a geological upheaval from deep within the bowels of the earth, the crystalline rocks of Iona are infinitely older than its neighbouring islands; in fact, they are possibly the oldest in the world.

I have found that the subtle energy fields emitted by certain rocks and their geological layers influence the senses of man and lead to a sensation of otherworldliness. This feeling is particularly enhanced and nourished when the strata are surrounded by water, hence the reason the Ancients chose these islands for their ceremonial practices and the burying of their dead.

Between Iona and the Isle of Man, the line I had discovered also passes through the Isle of Colonsay, another Druid centre of worship. A ring of megaliths on the east of the island called the Druids' Circle is the only remnant of their presence. Later the isle became the first centre in Scotland of Norsemen government.[13]

Geographically the Isle of Man is at the centre of the British Isles, and was one of the chief centres of the British Druids. The children of Celtic chiefs travelled to the colleges there for a full education in the teachings of the Druids.[14] Anglesey was another Druidical educational centre for the local rulers of Wales and northern England. Tacitus tells us that Anglesey was their chief religious centre.[5] Archaeology has confirmed these traditions with the discovery on the island of over a hundred votive objects dating from the first century AD, found in the soil of a dried-up lake.[14] (Votive means a revered or consecrated offering given voluntarily for a sacred purpose. In other words, the votive offerings were sacred

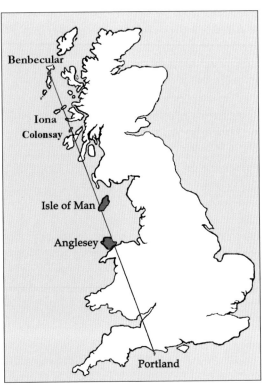

*An alignment of sacred isles.*

objects offered to the Lake Spirit on Anglesey when a lake existed in Roman times.) After the Druids converted to Christianity, Anglesey continued to be a place of education for the new religion, until their massacre by the Romans.

I discovered that historical legends link three of these islands. The legendary Bran was one of three children of King Lyr. His sister, Branwen, was buried on Anglesey and his brother, Manawyddan, was Lord and Protector of the Isle of Man.[15] Iona was also the seat of the Arch Druid of Britain and Bran was said to be the last Arch Druid.

The recent archaeological excavations on the playing fields south of St George's Church (see photo in Walk 5) revealed circular buildings dating from the Roman period. Round buildings are more common to early Christian and Culdee (later Druidic) sites, such as those found in Wales, Scotland and Ireland.

I feel that this remarkable alignment is more than a coincidence. The fact that Portland lies at the base of a string of major Druid religious centres of education may indicate the former importance of this isle. I can only conclude that this is yet another of the many wonderful mysteries of Portland.

# Conclusion

Today, Portland is experiencing considerable change due to the forthcoming Olympics in 2012. This will undoubtedly bring a new generation of people to the island, breathing life into some of the dilapidated areas, creating with it new shops, galleries and cafés. Eventually the old quarries will serve a new purpose, becoming recreational learning centres – like Tout Quarry Sculpture Park and another proposed at Independant Quarry. The day will come when people purposely visit the island to learn of and experience the beneficial qualities of Portland stone.

I believe that Portland has been a hallowed place for many people over thousands of years. Its former inhabitants created a sacred landscape with the building of mounds, stone circles, churches and sacred geometry, not only to honour their gods and goddesses but also to enhance the well-being and spiritual growth of Portland's people.

On my many visits to the island churches, I could not help noticing the uplifting atmosphere during the services and the friendliness of the locals. I believe there are two reasons for this. First, the harmonising effect of the Portland sacred geometry radiates through the fabric of the churches, and, second, and most importantly, the 'Spirit of Portland' continues to live through the islanders.

My experience of Portland has been remarkable in many ways and I feel that in addition to the already-recognised role the isle has played in British history, there should be some recognition of her sacredness. Perhaps as more people begin to experience the island as I have, they will also appreciate this quality and sense the ancient 'Spirit of Portland'.

# Appendix A

# A Walking Guide to Portland's Sacred Sites and Folklore

The spectacular, wild and rugged coastline of Portland is perfectly suited for ramblers of all ages to explore. All five walks are within the capabilities of anyone with average fitness as there are relatively few hills and most of the footpaths are clearly marked. However, there may be certain areas that could be slippery when wet and in places loose stones make walking awkward, so good walking shoes are essential.

Remarkably, there has been in the last couple of years a vast improvement to the landscape of the island with the removal of unsightly rusting containers and wrecked cars, particularly around Nicodemus Knob and the Grove. Many of the old quarries are now habitats for rare species of wild flowers, grasses, moths and butterflies and are ablaze with colour in spring and summer.

Although much of Portland's ancient history has visually disappeared through quarrying, the walks will introduce you to a sacred landscape consisting of old and new sacred sites such as churches, holy wells and sacred rocks. Through the writings of old Portlanders and travelling antiquarians, and most importantly place names that record the island's illustrious past, I have marked on the maps the sites where the old stone monuments possibly once stood and have indicated where the remnants of them can still be seen preserved in the walls.

Because none of the walks are very long you can incorporate one or two of them to make longer walks, particularly those that take in the upper part of the island. Portland is changing all the time and so some of the paths described in the walks may alter after publication. I also recommend using Ordnance Survey Map OL15 to complement the schematic maps.

Refreshments are available on all the walks with cafés at Chiswell, Easton and the Bill as well as numerous pubs dotted around the island. For those who prefer a picnic lunch there are shops in Easton and Weston.

I have specifically designed these walking tours for the individual or group to explore the unique diversity of Portland, and to connect with the special nature and spirit of the land.

# Walk 1
# Rufus Castle and God's Acre

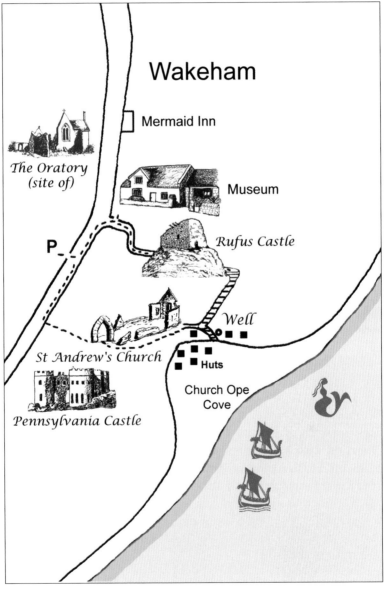

*Approx. 1 mile, on steep and rough path after Rufus Castle.*

From the parking area opposite Pennsylvania Castle, walk across the road to the thatched museum. Here you can see some of the objects of interest mentioned earlier in the book, such as the unusual stone sarcophagi and enigmatic stone head, along with some beautifully carved stones from the Norman church of St Andrew. The cottages that house the Museum were donated to the people of Portland in 1930 by Dr Marie Stopes, a pioneer of birth control in Britain. The end house, once called Avice's Cottage, is mentioned in Thomas Hardy's novel *The Well-Beloved*.

On the opposite side of the road are some modern houses, once the site of the Oratory or Vicar's house, which contained important historical records of the island until Cromwell's forces burnt down the building.

Outside the front of the museum are some fossilised remains of prehistoric trees. On a gate next to the museum is the name Maypole Meadow, a reminder that this site was a place of spring festivals. The celebrations may have taken place within the grounds of Rufus Castle, when a moat existed here in the nineteenth century.

Take the lane leading towards Rufus Castle. From the viewing platform below the castle, a path and steps lead down to Church Ope Cove. At the bottom of the steps before you arrive at the beach is an old well set amongst the beach huts next to the water tap. As you stand on the beach looking out to

*Church Ope Cove and Rufus Castle.*

sea, imagine that this cove was once part of the land that slipped into the sea in AD 1099.

Go back up the hill and take the old steps on your left up to the ruin of St Andrew's Church. A short way up here a small track on the right goes to an opening in the rock beneath Rufus Castle. This low tunnel leads to a stone-pillared chamber that may have been a Roman reservoir. It is not advisable to venture into this place, as many of the caves on Portland are dangerous to enter unless you have the right equipment.

The ruined church of St Andrew, once called 'God's Acre', is the sacred centre of Portland. At the northern end, where the high altar once stood, three island churches are equidistant from this very spot. Look amongst the gravestones and table tombs to find carvings of skull and bones, important Masonic emblems, which represent the transience of the material world and initiation for a symbolic rebirth.

Another path leads you through a Gothic arch, the remains of a tower mysteriously separated from the church. Continue along the path that rises steeply through the woods, past Pennsylvania Castle, to the main road. Opposite is the parking area at the start of the walk.

# Walk 2
# Giants, Megaliths and the Grove

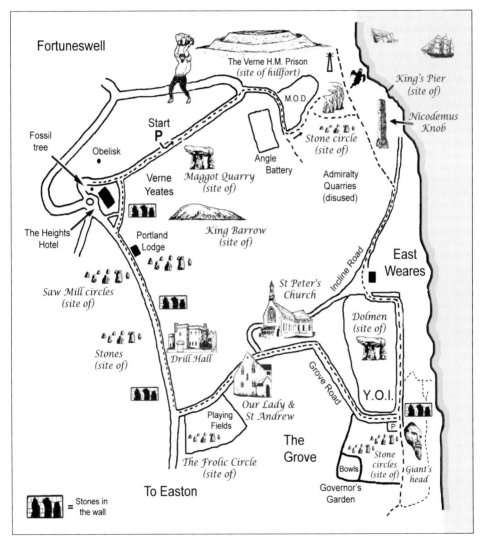

*Approx. 4 miles (without detour), on relatively flat roads and good paths.*
*The detour to view the giant's head adds approx. ⅔ mile, on steep, rough paths.*

According to the old Portlanders, the area between the Heights Hotel and Easton, including the Grove, was once rich in prehistoric temples and Druidical remains before quarrying destroyed them. This walk guides you around these megalithic sites, including the magnificent St Peter's Church, and you will see remnants of the old stones and where they once stood.

**The parking area opposite the Heights Hotel is a good place to start,** with magnificent views of Chesil Beach and the coast of Dorset. Here the devil allegedly played quoits across to Hardy's Monument in the distance. **Walking east towards the Verne Citadel** (now a prison) you can view the great ditches that form the defences of the fort, built by convicts between 1860 and 1887. This site was once a double-banked Iron Age hillfort inhabited by the Slingers.

**Follow the road past the prison entrance on the left until it ends; then go left along the perimeter fence until you reach the cliff. An overgrown path leads left along Undercliff Walk and peters out just past the transmitter.** This is a place of ghostly sounds, as described in Chapter 2.

**Go back and head south until you see a freestanding rock pillar by the coast** called Nicodemus Knob.

**Past this and along the tarmac road (Incline Road),** you approach the Young Offenders Institution, formerly Portland Prison. This is the site of megalithic circles and a dolmen, which nineteenth century locals avoided because of the stories of human sacrifice by Druid priests. (A dolmen is the French word widely used for a megalithic chambered tomb consisting of a large flat stone elevated by upright stones. One exists intact in Dorset below Hardy's Monument called 'The Hell Stone'. Lanyon Quoit is a famous example in Cornwall. See http://www.stonepages.com/england/lanyonquoit. html for a good example of how the Portland dolmens looked. The stones were originally covered with earth, but over the years they have lost their covering.)

**Follow the Coast Path until you come to Grove Road.** Here in the wall opposite Grove Road are large stones that may be remnants of a circle or dolmen. As mentioned earlier, Elizabeth Pearce describes a natural phenomenon at the Grove: "… when the moon rises red across St Alban's Head the first rays fall athwart this place". Megalithic priests may have built monuments here to honour the first light of the moon, capturing it within the circles.

Along the coast below the Y.O.I. are the remains of some old piers from which quarried stone was loaded onto boats. **For those without walking difficulties, a steep narrow signposted path about 50 yards back along the walls of the Y.O.I. leads down to the Weares.** Looking up from the lower path, a giant's head carved by nature and quarrying peers down at you from above. The head is below the old stones set in the wall opposite Grove Road.

Continue along this lower path to rejoin the main route, just south of the bowling green.

If you don't take the detour to see the giant's head, continue along the upper Coast Path past the Visitor's car park until you see the bowling green. According to King Warry, somewhere in this vicinity a circle of stones had part fallen over the edge to the Weares below in late Victorian times.

Retrace your steps and take Grove Road towards Easton past the Prison Governor's garden (which may be open for viewing) until you arrive at the Romanesque church of St Peter, built from the finest local stone in the Byzantine style of the twelfth century and filled with Masonic symbols. This was probably the site of the earliest church on the island. The remains of a medieval building, possibly a church or settlement, came to light during an archaeological excavation in the grounds of the Old Vicarage next door to the church. Sadly, many years of neglect and abandonment have taken their toll on the church. However, the new owner is restoring the building to allow the public to make use of it, with art exhibitions and other events planned for the future. The walled road that curves behind St Peter's and the Vicarage (Incline Road) may mark the outline of an earlier circular enclosure or estate.

A little further along the road to Easton, set within a row of terraced houses, is the Roman Catholic Church of Our Lady and St Andrew, built in 1868.

Also along this road are playing fields, the site of a circular enclosure containing standing stones called by locals 'The Frolic'.

Turning north along Easton Lane you come to a castled Victorian building called the Drill Hall, originally built for the Portland Volunteer Artillery Brigade in 1868.

Just after the Drill Hall there used to be a public house called the Saw Mill Tavern. Two stone circles were seen here in the nineteenth century by Elizabeth Pearce standing either side of the old road; one of them stood behind the Tavern, the other on the verge by the quarry opposite. King Warry also saw the remains of these circles and noted that they may have had some ceremonial or astronomical purpose, because if you draw a line from the old harbour (now the Osprey Quay) to St Andrew's Church at Church Ope Cove it passes between them. The walls along Easton Lane near to where the Tavern once stood contain ancient weathered stones, probably the megaliths of these circles preserved by the superstitious quarrymen.

Continue walking to the Heights Hotel and turn into a road behind the hotel. More old megaliths set between modern stones lie in the walls here. At the obelisk north of the hotel, we stand in a moot place, an area where meetings were held in ancient times. A deep natural chasm from Verne Hill to the land south of here gave the vicinity its name, Yeates, from the Old English word for 'gap'. **A fossilised tree stands in the grounds of the hotel** taken from one of the nearby quarries.

*Fossilised tree at the Heights Hotel.*

# Walk 3
# Witches, Holy Wells and a Sea Monster

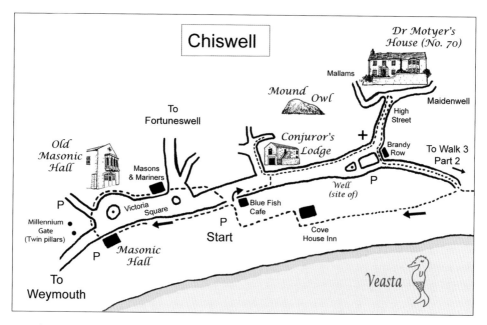

*Total walk approx. 2 miles. Part 1 approx. 1¼ miles, on roads and paths. Part 2 approx. ¾ mile, on good paths, but rough along Hiram's Walk to the sacred rock.*

**This walk starts in Chiswell. Park by the Blue Fish Café close to Victoria Square**.

Chiswell is the oldest settlement on Portland, becoming the largest by the end of the eighteenth century. Ancient settlers founded the village between the old harbour known as the Mere and the bay at the end of Chesil Beach, as it was the ideal location for trade and fishing. The settlement has survived for centuries despite suffering from disastrous floods.

**From the car park, walk south along the main road until you reach Clements Lane on the left. The building on the corner** here has an external staircase leading to an upper room. It has the unusual name of Conjuror's Lodge because between 1816 and 1826 this room was used for worship by a breakaway group of island Methodists accused of practising witchcraft.[1]

**Behind and above the Lodge is a grassy knoll, best seen from just up**

Clements Lane. Folklore says this is a prehistoric mound called Mound Oel or Owl, although some authorities refer to it as Mount Howle.

**A short way up High Street you will see a large Queen Anne house (No. 70 Mallams) dating from 1750, called the Captain's House.** Some strange stories are associated with this building. The most interesting is the story of a Victorian resident called Dr Motyer who, like a witch doctor, prescribed remedies and potions to the sick. Some believe he was an alchemist, whose experiments struck fear into his neighbours. An account of this tale by Geoff Kirby published in the *Free Portland News* in August 1990 mentions that one evening sometime in March 1868, residents of Underhill experienced a mighty explosion. Incredibly, the blast removed the roof of the doctor's house, with just the badly damaged walls remaining. The next part of the story is truly amazing for the locals discovered gold dust in the streets around Chiswell, as if Dr Motyer had finally succeeded in what alchemists have been trying to achieve for centuries – turning base metal into gold. According to Kirby, the facts around this incident have been hard to prove, as the Underhill people kept the incident a secret from the Tophill folk so that they could claim the precious metal for themselves. The house remained empty without a roof for over 100 years, until 1997 when it was restored to its former glory.

**Back down the road and left towards the beach** are some old stone cottages in Brandy Row; many of these houses were flooded in the great storm of 1824 and more recently in 1990.

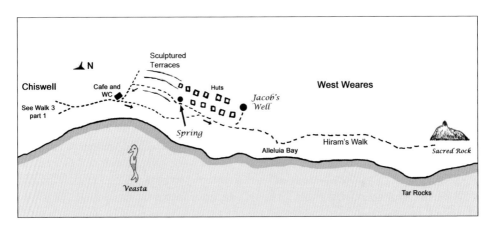

**A path along the West Weares known as Hiram's Walk takes you past beach huts to Jacob's Well,** formerly Silver Well. The trail weaves its way through the Weares along a difficult eroded path, with the sea on one side and the towering cliffs on the other. Hiram painted and carved religious texts on the rocks. Unfortunately, most of the inscriptions are no longer visible due to erosion, except for one stone which until recently depicted the single word Jessu, until someone thoughtlessly carved it into Jessica.

At the end of the path is an enigmatic boulder on a knoll; this rock may have been here for thousands of years and has a strong presence of sacredness, as do similar rocks in Cornwall and other parts of Britain.

Returning to the huts, take the path towards the field sculpture terraces and on your right is another spring.

As you walk back to Chiswell look out to sea for Veasta, Portland's very own sea monster. This 12-ft-tall creature has the head of a crested sea horse and the torso of a fish. Veasta has made occasional appearances off the shores of the island over a period spanning five centuries, recently in 1995 and on the day of the solar eclipse in 1999.[2] (See M.J. Ball's account on www.weymouth.gov. uk.) Perhaps the legendary mermaid from Church Ope Cove may have been Veasta.

In the summer of 2002, Chesil Cove was the scene of another unusual event. A lone dolphin arrived in the cove and stayed for weeks. As soon as the news spread of a friendly dolphin at Portland, hundreds of people arrived to see and swim with him. He is called Georges in France and Randy in the Channel Islands and has been spotted around the Dorset coast for years. I personally witnessed the joy this dolphin gave to people who swam with him. Despite warning signs put up by the council that it is dangerous to swim with wild dolphins, I entered the water and touched this magnificent creature, an unforgettable event.

Take the turning just after Cove House Inn, then turn left and follow the road back to the car park. Back at the main road, turn left into Victoria Square and past the Masonic Hall. Here are two pillars, a significant symbol of the Masons, erected as a Millennium Gate to Portland.

On the other side of the road is the old Masonic Hall, now accommodation for divers. On the front of this building there are carvings of sacred geometry on the stone window surrounds and four Masonic lions beneath.

Return along the road to the parking area at the start of the walk.

*Veasta (next to Ferry Bridge Inn, Wyke Regis).*

# Walk 4
# Caves, Fairies and Black Dogs

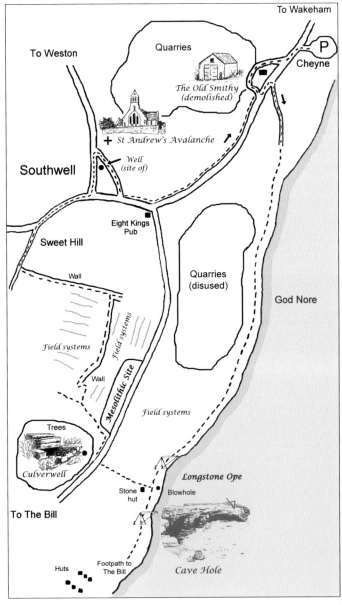

*Approx. 2½ miles, on roads and paths, but a little awkward from Culverwell to Sweet Hill.*

This walk begins at the parking area at Cheyne on the eastern side of the main road between Wakeham and Southwell.

Walk a little south along the main road from the parking area and take the lane on the west side of the road that drops down to the entrance of a quarry. On the left of the lane just before the old rails in the track there once stood an old smithy or blacksmith's shop. According to folklore, the lane here, part of the original road to Southwell, is the haunt of strange lights and fairies.

*Walkers at the former Old Smithy.*

The village of Southwell is right at the heart of Portland folklore, and many of the old people in the village know of the little people or elementals, called 'Nanny Diamonds' and 'Necromancers'. They are said to dwell in the holes in the remnants of the walls that lead from the former Blacksmith's shop to the village. The 'Necromancers' are the helpers, good fairies who dress in green tunics and white cone-shaped hats with a feather stuck in the band. The 'Nanny Diamonds' wear short white dresses and white Phrygian hats and are mischievous sprites that have the power to put the evil eye on anyone who crosses their path. They still haunt this area at night, so beware.[3]

It is interesting that this fairy lane begins at the Smithy, for long ago metallurgy was a mysterious art that people associated with the divine, performed by the semi-divine blacksmith. Before the industrial revolution, the blacksmith was a very important figure in the community; his craft of melting iron ore and making tools, utensils and weapons was considered sacred. In the Indian Rigveda, the creator of the world was a blacksmith, and the Anglo-Saxons had a blacksmith god called Wayland.

**Continue on to the main road, turn left, then right and take the signposted Coast Path** which leads south to the Bill. **This route through the old cliff quarries** has splendid views of the Dorset coast. The headland you can see in the distance is St Alban's Head. When the moon rises from behind St Alban's Head the first rays cast their light over the Grove area. St Alban brought Masonic knowledge to England.

**The rusting, timber crane by a little bay** marks a quarry; its name Longstone Ope is a reminder of a fallen menhir or megalith that once stood in the vicinity.

**Just before the second rusting metal crane near the single stone hut,** look for a rocky depression in which lies an iron grill weighted down by large stones; this is a blowhole, an opening in the roof of a sea cavern.

**South of here is Cave Hole.** There are many caves on Portland and their entrances can be found in the quarries or on the coast, some at sea level, others halfway up the cliffs, formed when the sea rose in prehistoric times. Dogs have been utilised for centuries to provide a guide through the complicated cave systems. Their acute sense of smell gives them the ability to find their way back to the entrance.

*Cave Hole.*

Cave Hole has a legend attached to it, probably invented by the smugglers who used this place. It is the haunt of a black dog, the dreaded Roy Dog, supposed to be as big as a man, with large fiery eyes, one green, one red, and entwined in his shaggy dark fur can be seen the freshly plucked eyes of his victims. The creature emerges from the watery depths to seize any traveller passing by, and drags him or her down into his dark watery domain.[4] Black dogs are often associated with caves, which are said to be entrances to the underworld, and they occur in ancient cultures around the world as guardians of the underworld. In the Egyptian cult of the dead, a black jackal-headed dog Anubis guides the soul through the difficult journey in the underworld. In Greek mythology, one of the heads of the underworld goddess Hecate is that of a dog and she is associated with the Dog Star, Sirius. Her pet was the dog Cerberus who guarded the entrance to Hades.

For hundreds of years reports of ghostly black dogs have been the subject of folklore throughout the British Isles and Europe. At night they are seen in areas close to hallowed places or ley points, such as churchyards, prehistoric remains and ancient trackways. Sometimes they obstruct your way, like the other black dog apparition witnessed on Portland called the Row Dog.[5] This dog does not attack you, though he snarls and barks aggressively to keep you away from the secret he guards. What secret this may be is conjecture.

**Next, backtrack 50 yards to the single stone hut, then take the grassy track up to the main road, heading towards a patch of trees and bushes**. Here you will find the ancient Culverwell.

**After a short walk along the main road towards Southwell take the first footpath on the left signposted Sweet Hill**. On the right is the Mesolithic archaeological site open at certain times during the summer. This unique site gives an insight into how a small community lived here over 7000 years ago.[6]

The path can be confusing, but **cross the stile on your right and head left up the hill towards the stone wall. Turn right** which takes you across the ancient field strips that run in parallel between Southwell and Portland Bill. They date back to Saxon times when the strip farming system was common throughout Dorset and the south of England. Up until the Victorian era they existed all over Tophill, when they were destroyed by quarrying. The Portland system of land inheritance favoured both sexes of the family, and over the years the plots were divided and subdivided, so that later islanders ended up owning almost unworkable small strips of land. One of these once-cultivated rows, **to the right of the path along the ridge to Southwell**, may have contained the stone avenue referred to in Chapter 2, as two pairs of stones at different ends of this field are marked on old maps.

**At the junction, turn left to Sweet Hill. Turn right to Southwell, then take the left fork to St Andrew's Church**, built in 1879. Notice the axis of the church is unusually oriented to the north-west, to the old mother church of St Andrew's at Church Ope Cove. The triangular play area below the church was once the site of the village well, which gave Southwell its name.

**Take Church Lane back to the main road and head east past the Eight Kings Pub. Continue along the main road towards Wakeham until you reach the starting point**.

# Walk 5
## Churches on the Divine Plan

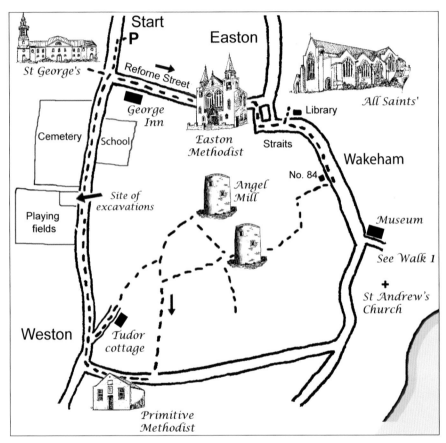

*Approx. 2¼ miles, flat, on roads and good paths.*

This walk takes you around the magnificent churches that feature in the island's geometry, starting at St George's Church, Reforne. I recommend a visit to both the Easton Methodist and All Saints' Churches, as they not only contain many wonders but also have the friendliest congregations I have ever met.

**You can park either at St George's Centre or in Reforne Street opposite the church.** Now run by volunteers, St George's opens May to October from 2–7 p.m., seven days a week. The church is a fine example of Georgian architecture influenced by Wren and built by Thomas Gilbert. **Inside the church**

a metal stud on the floor marks the spot where the circle of St Andrew passes under the dome. The meridian line, mentioned in Chapter 6, passes through the altar, above which is a memorial to Thomas Gilbert. The pentagonal line from Weston Chapel to the Jehovah's Witness Hall passes through the tower. The stairs up to the gallery take you past an unusual little room in the tower.

**Among the impressive graves in the churchyard** is a rather unusual Islamic-style tomb, situated along the northern side of the graveyard. Here is the resting place of two of the main characters who have inspired this book, Clara King Warry and her grandmother Elizabeth Pearce, descendants of the Whit Jutes whose distant ancestors may have originated from the Middle East.

*Tomb of Clara King Warry and Elizabeth Pearce.*

**Opposite the church along Reforne Street** is the George Inn where Court Leet meetings were held long ago and which displays one of the ancient Reeve staffs behind the bar. (There are more in the Portland Museum.)

**A short walk further along Reforne Street brings you to the Edwardian Easton Square and the impressive Easton Methodist Church** with the altar front depicting Leonardo da Vinci's Last Supper; unfortunately, the church is only accessible after services. Notice the fine carving of the Ascension above the main door. The neighbouring old Methodist School has a double Vesica in the window.

From the Square, continue towards Wakeham along a street called Straits. A witch lived in one of the cottages here and the Portland Museum displays a petrified cat found in the walls of her home, presumably to ward off evil spirits. **You will soon see a library on the left next to a driveway that leads to All Saints' Church**. Today, this grand Gothic building is the main parish church on the island, and full of mystery. It is the sacred 'Mark Point' where once stood a monument so important that the road was built around it. Inside, above the beautiful east window depicting the mythical Heavenly Twins, is the splendid painted signs of the zodiac, with a Green Man on one of the bosses (ornamental protuberances). An ancient 'Sun Cross' from the old mother church of St Andrew leans against the wall below the pulpit. Behind the altar are shields depicting the island saints and churches on the Vesica geometry. The new extension, called the Millennium Room, is a key place where sacred geometry lines cross.

**Continue along Straits and stroll down ancient picturesque Wakeham**, with its stone-built houses, some of which are probably medieval.

**At No. 84 take the footpath on the right between the houses**, which leads to the windmills at the centre of the island within the All-Seeing Eye. The northern windmill has the unusual name of Angel Mill.

**Continue west along the track and turn left. At the main road, turn right to the little Primitive Methodist Chapel at Weston**, so integral to the pentagonal geometry, but no longer in use. **The road north takes you past Gypsy Lane tucked away on the right**; a short walk down here brings you to a lovely thatched Tudor cottage, probably the oldest inhabited building on the island.

The main road has one other place of interest before you return to St George's Church. **The playing fields just below the cemetery** were the site of the archaeological excavations mentioned in Chapter 11.

*Foundations of a circular building at Weston Playing Fields.*

# Appendix B

# British Kings from Samothes to Ine[1]

| Line of Horus | Years ruled | Dates | |
|---|---|---|---|
| Samothes | 46 | 2094–2048 BC | |
| Magus | 51 | 2048–1997 | |
| Sarronius | 61 | 1997–1936 | |
| Druiyus | 14 | 1936–1922 | (founder of the Druids) |
| Bardus | 75 | 1922–1847 | |
| Longho | 28 | 1847–1819 | |
| Bardus II | 37 | 1819–1782 | |
| Lucus | 11 | 1782–1771 | |
| Celtes | 13 | 1771–1758 | |

| Line of Hercules | Years ruled | Dates | |
|---|---|---|---|
| Albion | (unknown) | | (invaded Britain) |
| Hercules | 19 | 1758–1739 | (defeated Albion) |
| Galates | 49 | 1739–1690 | |
| Harbon | 18 | 1690–1672 | |
| Lugdus | 51 | 1672–1621 | |
| Beligius | 20 | 1621–1601 | |
| Iasius | 50 | 1601–1551 | |
| Allobrox | 68 | 1551–1483 | |
| Romus | 29 | 1483–1454 | |
| Paris | 39 | 1454–1415 | |
| Lemanus | 62 | 1415–1353 | |
| Olbius | 5 | 1353–1348 | |
| Galates II | 48 | 1348–1300 | |
| Nannes | 44 | 1300–1256 | |
| Remis | 40 | 1256–1216 | |
| Francus | 67 | 1216–1149 | |
| Pictus | | 1149 | (defeated by Trojan Brutus) |

| Trojan Britons | Years ruled | Dates |
|---|---|---|
| Brutus | 24 | 1149–1125 |
| Locrine | 20 | 1125–1105 |
| Madan | 40 | 1105–1065 |
| Mempricius | 20 | 1065–1045 |
| Ebranck | 40 | 1045–1005 |
| Brute II | 12 | 1005–993 |
| Leil | 25 | 993–968 |
| Lud | 39 | 968–929 |
| Baldud | 20 | 929–909 |
| Leir | 60 | 909–849 |
| Cordeilla (Queen) | 5 | 849–844 |
| Cunedag and Margan | 33 | 844–811 |
| Rival | 46 | 811–765 |
| Gurgust | 84 | 765–681 |
| Silvius | 49 | 681–632 |
| Jago | 28 | 632–604 |
| Kimmacus | 54 | 604–550 |
| Gorbodug | 63 | 550–487 |
| Ferrex and Porrex | 5 | 487–482 |

After the death of Porrex and Ferrex the land of Britain was divided among Rudaucus, king of Wales, Clotenus, king of Cornwall, Pinor, king of Loegria, Statorius, king of Albania, and Yevan, king of Northumberland, for 48 years (482–434). (Source http://www.keithhunt.com/Britain2.html.)

| | | | |
|---|---|---|---|
| Molmutius | 40 | 434–394 | |
| Belinus and Brennus | 22 | 394–372 | |
| Gurguint | 19 | 372–353 | |
| Guintelyn | 26 | 353–327 | |
| Silvius II | 15 | 327–312 | |
| Kimarus | 3 | 312–309 | |
| Elanius or Danius | 10 | 309–299 | |
| Morindus | 9 | 299–290 | |
| Gorboman | 10 | 290–280 | |
| Archigallo | 1 | 280–279 | |
| Elidure (brother) | 3 | 279–276 | |
| Archigallo | 10 | 276–266 | (restored to the throne) |
| Elidure | 1 | 266–265 | (restored to the throne) |
| Vigenius and Peridurus | 9 | 265–256 | |
| Elidure | 4 | 256–252 | (restored to the throne) |
| Gorbonian | 10 | 252–242 | |
| Morgan | 14 | 242–228 | |
| Emerianus | 7 | 228–221 | |
| Ydwallo | 20 | 221–201 | |

| Trojan Britons | Years ruled | Dates |
|---|---|---|
| Rimo | 16 | 201–185 |
| Geruntius | 20 | 185–165 |
| Gatellus | 10 | 165–155 |
| Coilus | 10 | 155–145 |
| Perrox II | 5 | 145–140 |
| Cherimus | 1 | 140–139 |
| Fulgentius | 1 | 139–138 |
| Eldred | 1 | 138–137 |
| Androgeus | 1 | 137–136 |
| Urianus | 3 | 136–133 |
| E Elihud | 5 | 133–128 |
| Dedantius | 5 | 128–123 |
| Detonus | 2 | 123–121 |
| Gurguineus | 3 | 121–118 |
| Merianus | 2 | 118–116 |
| Bladud | 2 | 116–114 |
| Capenus | 3 | 114–111 |
| Ovinus | 2 | 111–109 |
| Sisilius | 2 | 109–107 |
| Bledgabedrus | 10 | 107–97 |
| Archimalus | 2 | 97–95 |
| Eldolus | 4 | 95–91 |
| Rodianus | 2 | 91–89 |
| Redargius | 3 | 89–86 |
| Samulius | 2 | 86–84 |
| Penisillus | 3 | 84–81 |
| Phyrrus | 2 | 81–79 |
| Caporius | 2 | 79–77 |
| Dinellus | 4 | 77–73 |
| Heli | 1 | 73–72 |
| Lud | 11 | 72–61 |
| Cassivelaunus | 23 | 61–38 |
| Tenvantius | 20 | 38–18 |
| Cunobelinus | 30 | 18 BC to AD 12 |
| Caractacus | 31 | 12–43 |
| Arvirargus | 14 | 43–57 |
| Marius | 40 | 57–97 |
| Coilus | 40 | 97–137 |
| Lucius | 49 | 137–186 |
| Geta | 35 | 186–221 |
| Bassianus | 35 | 221–256 |
| Caruasius | 40 | 256–296 |
| Asclepiodotus | 10 | 296–306 |
| Coel | 3 | 306–309 |

| Trojan Britons | Years ruled | Dates | |
|---|---|---|---|
| Constantius | 3 | 309–312 | |
| Constantine I | 25 | 312–337 | |
| Octavius I | 5 | 330–335 | |
| Octavius II | 13 | 335–348 | |
| Maximianus | 14 | 348–362 | |
| Caradocus | 13 | 362–375 | |
| Dionotus | 14 | 375–389 | |
| Gracianus | 13 | 389–402 | |
| Constantine II | 18 | 402–420 | |
| Constans | 17 | 420–437 | |
| Vortigern | 18 | 437–455 | |
| Vortimer | 5 | 455–460 | |
| Vortigern | 20 | 460–480 | (restored to the throne) |
| Aurellus Ambrosius | 21 | 480–501 | |
| Uther Pendragon | 20 | 501–521 | |
| Arthur | 21 | 521–542 | |
| Constantine III | 4 | 542–546 | |
| Aurellius Conanus | 3 | 546–549 | |
| Vortiporius | 1 | 549–550 | |
| Maelgwn | 5 | 550–555 | |
| Keredic | 8 | 555–563 | |
| Three unnamed kings | 53 | 563–616 | |
| Cadvan | 9 | 616–625 | |
| Cadwallo | 8 | 625–633 | |
| Cadwaller | 10 | 633–643 | |
| *Court fled to Brittany for 11 years* | | *(643–654)* | *because of famine* |
| Caedwalla | 10 | 654–664 | |
| Yvor | 39 | 664–703 | |
| Yni (Ine) | 36 | 688–724 | (ruled jointly with Yvor) |

# References and Bibliography

**Introduction**

[1]  Bromwich, R. (1961) *The Welsh Triads*. University of Wales Press, Cardiff.

**Chapter 1**

[1]  Francis, J. and Palmer, T. (2005) *Portland Quarries and Stone – The Geologists' View*. Portland Sculpture and Quarry Trust, http://learningstone.org/gv.html.

[2]  Callahan, P.S. (1984) *Ancient Mysteries, Modern Visions*. Acres, Kansas City.

[3]  Devereux, P. (1992) *Symbolic Landscapes*. Gothic Image Publications, Glastonbury.

[4]  Graves, T. (1978, 1986) *Needles of Stone*. Gothic Image Publications, Glastonbury.

[5]  Reich, W. (ed.) (1960) *Wilhelm Reich: Selected Writings*. Noonday Press, New York.

[6]  Warry, King, C. (*c* 1908) *The High Place*. Unpublished Box 1. Dorset County Museum, Dorchester.

**Chapter 2**

[1]  Warry, King, C. (1902) *Old Portland Traditions*. Dorset County Museum, Dorchester.

[2]  Warry, King, C. (*c* 1908) *The High Place*. Unpublished Box 1. Dorset County Museum, Dorchester.

[3]  Lunettes, F. (1825) *An Historical and Descriptive Account of the Peninsula of Portland from the Earliest to the Present Times*. S. McDowell, Leadenhall, London.

[4]  Callahan, P.S. (1984) *Ancient Mysteries, Modern Visions*. Acres, Kansas City.

[5]  Pearce, White, E., White, King Warry, C.J., Edwards, J.M. and Legg, R. (1983) *Old Portland*. Dorset Publishing Company, Wincanton.

[6]  Legg, R. (1987) *Mysterious Dorset*. Dorset Publishing Company, Wincanton.

[7]  Palmer, S. (2005) *Portland Archaeological Inventory of Sites and Finds*. Susann Palmer, Portland.

[8]  Hardy, T. (1998) *The Well-Beloved (Oxford World's Classics Series)*. Oxford University Press, Oxford.

[9]  Morris, S. (1985) *Portland, An Illustrated History*. Dovecote Press, Wimborne.

[10]  Bromwich, R. (1961) *The Welsh Triads*. University of Wales Press, Cardiff.

[11]  Gordon, E.O. (1932) *Prehistoric London, Its Mounds and Circles*. Covenant Publishing, London.

[12]  Jowett, G.F. (1996) *The Drama of the Lost Disciples*. Covenant Publishing, London.

[13]  Protheroe, A.H.P. (1998) *A Voice at Culverwell*. Aspen Publishers, Portland.

## Chapter 3

1. Pearce, White, E., White, King Warry, C.J., Edwards, J.M. and Legg, R. (1983) *Old Portland*. Dorset Publishing Company, Wincanton.
2. Ingram, J. (translator) (1912) *The Anglo-Saxon Chronicle*. Everyman Press, London.
3. Dumville, D. (2003) *Bede: Ecclesiastical History of the English People*, translated by L. Shirly-Price and D. Farmer. Revised edn. Penguin Classics, London.
4. Hutchins, J. (1774) *History and Antiquities of the County of Dorset* (eds W. Shipp and J.W. Hodson), 3rd edn. J.B. Nichols and Sons, Westminster.
5. Weymouth and Portland Borough Council Leisure Department (1991) *Rufus Castle*. Museums Service Publication, Portland Museum.
6. Grose, F. (1783) *Antiquities of England and Wales*. C. Clarke, for S. Hooper, London.
7. Warry, King, C. (1902) *Old Portland Traditions*. Dorset County Museum, Dorchester.
8. Warry, King, C. (*c* 1908) *The High Place*. Unpublished Box 1, Dorset County Museum, Dorchester.
9. Britannia Internet Magazine (1997) *The Anglo Saxon Chronicle*. http://www.britannia.com/history/docs/1095-99.html.
10. Bohn, A.M. (1854) *The Chronicle of Florence of Worcester* (translated by Thomas Forester). Henry G. Bohn, London.
11. Stow, J. (1580) *Chronicles of England*. Henry Bynneman, for Ralphe Newberie, London.
12. Answers Corporation (2009) *Goodwin Sands*. http://www.answers.com/topic/goodwin-sands.
13. Pennick, N. (1997) *Lost Cities and Sunken Lands*. Capall Bann Publishing, Milverton.
14. Searle, A. (1998) *Isle of Wight Folklore*. Dovecote Press, Wimborne.
15. Loader, R. and Tomalin, D. (1997) *Time and Tide*. Isle of Wight Council and English Heritage.
16. Moss, V. (1993) *The Saints of Anglo-Saxon England*, vol. II. op. cit., pp. 42–52. Saint Nectarios Press, Seattle.
17. Morris, S. (1985) *Portland, An Illustrated History*. Dovecote Press, Wimborne.
18. *The Winchester Chronicle*. Cotton MS otho B xi, 2. British Library, London.
19. Knight, C. and Lomas, R. (1999) *Uriel's Machine, the Prehistoric Technology that Survived the Flood*. Century Books, London.
20. Pearce, R. (1898) *Methodism in Portland and a Page of Church History*. Charles H. Kelly, London.
21. Harte, J. (1998) *Legends*. Dovecote Press, Wimborne.
22. Waring, E. (1977) *Ghosts and Legends of the Dorset Countryside*. Compton Press, Tisbury.

## Chapter 4

1. Michell, J. (1994) *At the Centre of the World: Polar Symbolism Discovered in Celtic, Norse and Other Ritualized Landscapes*. Thames and Hudson, London.
2. Michell, J. (1983) *The New View Over Atlantis*. Thames and Hudson, London.
3. Watkins, A. (1925, 1974) *The Old Straight Track*. Abacus, London.
4. Pennick, N. (1994) *Sacred Geometry*. Capall Bann Publishing, Milverton.
5. Warry, King, C. (1902) *Old Portland Traditions*. Dorset County Museum,

Dorchester.

6   Mackenzie, R. (1993) *Portland: A Topographical and Historical Gazetteer.* K.D. Print, Wells.

7   Harvey, P.E.G. (1978) *900 Years in the Life of a Fortress Isle.* Portland 900 Years Committee.

8   Palmer, S. (2005) *Portland Archaeological Inventory of Sites and Finds.* Susann Palmer, Portland.

9   Morris, S. (1985) *Portland, An Illustrated History.* Dovecote Press, Wimborne.

10  Leyland, J. (1535–1543) *The Itinerary of John Leyland In Or About the Years 1535–1543.* Bibliobazaar, Charleston, South Carolina.

11  Lunettes, F. (1825) *An Historical and Descriptive Account of the Peninsula of Portland from the Earliest to the Present Times.* S. McDowell, Leadenhall, London.

12  Warry, King, C. (*c* 1908) *The High Place.* Unpublished Box 1. Dorset County Museum, Dorchester.

13  Pearce, R. (1898) *Methodism in Portland and a Page of Church History.* Charles H. Kelly, London.

14  Insole, A.V. (1952) *Immortal Britain.* The Aquarian Press, London.

15  Waddell, L.A. (1924) *The Phoenician Origin of Britons, Scots and Anglo-Saxons.* Williams and Norgate, London. Reprinted 1990 by Banton Press, Largs.

**Chapter 5**

1   Pennick, N. (1994) *Sacred Geometry.* Capall Bann Publishing, Milverton.

2   Gest, K.L. (2007) *The Secrets of Solomon's Temple.* Lewis Masonic, Hinckley.

3   Hancock, G. and Bauval, R. (2004) *Talisman Sacred Cities, Secret Faith.* Anchor Canada/Random House, Toronto.

4   Pearce, White, E., White, King Warry, C.J., Edwards, J.M. and Legg, R. (1983) *Old Portland.* Dorset Publishing Company, Wincanton.

5   Gardner, L. (2005) *The Shadow of Solomon: The Lost Secrets of the Freemasons Revealed.* Harper Element, London.

6   Baigent, M. and Leigh, R. (1989) *The Temple and the Lodge.* Arrow Books, London.

7   Warry, King, C. (*c* 1908) *The High Place.* Unpublished Box 1. Dorset County Museum, Dorchester.

8   Gilbert, A. (2002) *The New Jerusalem. Rebuilding London: The Great Fire, Christopher Wren and the Royal Society.* Bantam Press, London.

9   Wren, C. (son of) (1645–1747) *Parentalia: or, Memoirs of the Family of the Wrens.* T. Osborn and R. Dodsley, London.

10  Ricketts, E. (1979) *The Buildings of Old Portland.* Eric Ricketts, Portland.

11  Bettey, J.H. (1970) *The Island and Royal Manor of Portland, 1750–1851.* Court Leet of the Island and Royal Manor of Portland /University of Bristol.

12  *The Royal Commission on the Ancient Historical Monuments, Volume 2.* Dorset Records Office, Dorchester.

13  Knoop, D. and Jones, G.P. (1935) *The London Mason in the 17th Century.* Guildhall Press, London.

14  Condor, E. (1894) *The Hole Craft and Fellowship of Masons.* Masonic Book Club, Bloomington.

15  Schnoebelen, W. (1991) *Masonry: Beyond the Light.* Chick Publications, Ontario, California.

## Chapter 6

1. Warry, King, C. (c 1908) *The High Place*. Unpublished Box 1. Dorset County Museum, Dorchester.
2. Lawlor, R. (1982) *Sacred Geometry*. Thames and Hudson, London.
3. Pennick, N. (1994) *Sacred Geometry*. Capall Bann Publishing, Milverton.
4. Pearce, White, E., White, King Warry, C.J., Edwards, J.M. and Legg, R. (1983) *Old Portland*. Dorset Publishing Company, Wincanton.
5. Harvey, P.E.G. (1978) *900 Years in the Life of a Fortress Isle*. Portland 900 Years Committee.
6. Jordan, D.J. (undated) *Sacred Geometry of the Squared Circle*. http://www.geocities.com/davidjayjordan/squaredcircle.html.
7. Michell, J. (1988) *The Dimensions of Paradise.* Thames and Hudson, London.
8. Velikovsky, I. (1950) *Worlds in Collision*. Victor Gollancz, London.
9. Hardy, T. (1998) *The Well-Beloved (Oxford World's Classics Series)*. Oxford University Press, Oxford.

## Chapter 7

1. Pearce, White, E., White, King Warry, C.J., Edwards, J.M. and Legg, R. (1983) *Old Portland*. Dorset Publishing Company, Wincanton.
2. Waring, E. (1977) *Ghosts and Legends of the Dorset Countryside*. Compton Press, Tisbury.
3. Hymas, M. (1981) *Dorset Folklore*. Books of Wessex, Taunton.
4. Leek, S. (1976) *A Ring of Magic Islands*. American Photographic Book Publishing, New York.
5. Bromwich, R. (1961) *The Welsh Triads*. University of Wales Press, Cardiff.
6. Gordon, E.O. (1932) *Prehistoric London, Its Mounds and Circles*. Covenant Publishing, London.
7. Elder, I.H. (1962) *Celt, Druid and Culdee*. Covenant Publishing, London.
8. Caesar, Julius (100–44 BC) *De Bello Gallico. Book V1*. http://www.gutenberg.org/etext/10657.
9. Murphy, T. (2004) *Natural History: The Empire in the Encyclopedia*. Oxford University Press, Oxford.
10. Searle, A. (1998) *Isle of Wight Folklore*. Dovecote Press, Wimborne.
11. Knight, P. (1998) *Sacred Dorset – On the Path of the Dragon*. Capall Bann Publishing, Milverton.
12. Palmer, S. (1998) *Ancient Portland – Archaeology of the Isle*. Susann Palmer, Portland.
13. Savli, J., Bor, M. and Tomazic, I. (1980) *Veneti. First Builders of European Community*. http://www.angelfire.com/country/veneti/venetibookorderinfo.html.
14. Pääbo, A. (2003–2008) *The 'Veneti' Traders of Early Europe: 'Phoenicians of the Interior'?* http://www.paabo.ca/uirala/veneti.html.
15. Waddell, L.A. (1924) *The Phoenician Origin of Britons, Scots and Anglo-Saxons*. Williams and Norgate, London. Reprinted 1990 by Banton Press, Largs.
16. Pearce, S. (1949) *A Portland Vase*. Sarah Pearce, Portland.
17. Pearce, R. (1898) *Methodism in Portland and a Page of Church History*. Charles H. Kelly, London.
18. Hutchins, J. (1774) *History and Antiquities of the County of Dorset* (eds W. Shipp and J.W. Hodson), 3rd edn. J.B. Nichols, Westminster.
19. Morris, S. (1985) *Portland, An Illustrated History*. Dovecote Press, Wimborne.

20   Anonymous (1861) *Angels, Cherubim, and Gods*. Wertheim, London. Cited in Udal, J.S. (1989) *Dorsetshire Folklore*, 1922, pp. 120–121 in notes, 3rd edn. Dorset Books (an imprint of Wheaton Publishers), Exeter.

21   *Ancient Hebrew Sea Migrations*. Vol. 1, No. 3, July–September 1999. Official Journal of the Ensign Trust, http://www.ensignmessage.com/archives/sea.html.

22   Cunliffe, B. (2002) *The Extraordinary Voyage of Pytheas the Greek: The Man Who Discovered Britain*. Walker Publishing, New York.

23   Eardley-Wilmot, H. (1995) *The Overland Way: From Porlock to Portland in the Bronze Age? An Investigation*. Westcountry Books, Tiverton.

24   Warry, King, C. (1902) *Old Portland Traditions*. Dorset County Museum, Dorchester.

25   Stukeley, W. (1764) *Minute Book* for 5 March (Vol. 9, p. 233). Society of Antiquaries, London.

26   Beaumont, C. (1945) *The Riddle of Prehistoric Britain*. Rider, London.

27   Taylor, C. and Keen, L. (1999) *St Catherine's Chapel at Abbotsbury and the Legend of the Saint*. Abbotsbury Music Festival, Abbotsbury.

28   *The Bible*. Matthew 4:19.

29   Oliver, C. (undated) *Myths and Legends of the Saxon Saints of Wimborne*. C. Oliver, Wimborne.

30   Brown, M. (1990) *Dorset Customs, Curiosities & Country Lore*. Countryside Books, Newbury.

31   Udal, J.S. (1989) *Dorsetshire Folklore*, 1922, pp. 120–121 in notes, 3rd edn. Dorset Books (an imprint of Wheaton Publishers), Exeter.

32   Ingram, J. (translator) (1912) *The Anglo-Saxon Chronicle*. Everyman Press, London.

33   Nash, Ford, D. (2001) *Historical Chronology of the Early Saxon Kingdoms, Part 3: AD 693–755*. http://www.earlybritishkingdoms.com/adversaries/kingdoms/693.html.

34   Anonymous (2009) *Ine of Wessex*. http://en.wikipedia.org/wiki/ine_of_wessex.

35   Gibbs, R. (2000) *Ine, the First King of Wessex*. Llanerch Publishers, Felinfach.

36   Dumville, D. (2003) *Bede: Ecclesiastical History of the English People*, translated by L. Shirly-Price and D. Farmer. Penguin Classics, London.

37   Geoffrey of Monmouth (1984) *The History of the Kings of Britain*. Folio Society, London.

38   *Were the West Saxons guilty of ethnic cleansing?* Webpage Time Team Live 2001, Hampshire, 28–30 August. http://www.channel4.com/history/microsites/t/timeteam/archive/timeteamlive2001/feature_ethnic.html.

39   *New Advent St Ine*. http://www.newadvent.org/cathen/07789b.htm.

40   Myres, J.N.L. (1989) *The English Settlements (Oxford History of England)*. Oxford University Press, New York.

41   Raymond Capt, E. (1985) *Missing Links Discovered in Assyrian Tablets*. Artisan Publishers, Muskogee, Oklahoma.

42   *The Winchester Chronicle*. Cotton MS otho B xi, 2. British Library, London.

43   Mills, A.D. (1996) *The Place-Names of the Isle of Wight*. Paul Watkins, Stamford.

44   Higgins, G. (1992) *Anacalypsis – The Saitic Isis: Languages, Nations and Religions*. A & B Book Distributors, Brooklyn, New York.

45   House Shadow Drake (2007) http://www.traditionalwitchcraft.org/celtic/gundestrup.html.

## Chapter 8

[1]  *Were the West Saxons guilty of ethnic cleansing?* Webpage Time Team Live 2001, Hampshire, 28–30 August. http://www.channel4.com/history/microsites/t/timeteam/archive/timeteamlive2001/feature_ethnic.html.

[2]  Pennick, N. (1997) *Lost Cities and Sunken Lands.* Capall Bann Publishing, Milverton.

[3]  Baillie, M. (1999) *Exodus to Arthur: Catastrophic Encounters with Comets.* Batsford, London.

[4]  Morris, J. (1978) *Gildas: The Ruin of Britain and Other Documents.* Phillimore, London.

[5]  Rees, W.J. Rev. (ed.) (1840) *The Liber Landavensis.* The Welsh MSS Society, Llandovery.

[6]  Morris, J. (ed. and translator) (1980) *British History and the Welsh Annals.* Phillimore, London.

[7]  Ingram, J. (translator) (1912) *The Anglo-Saxon Chronicle.* Everyman Press, London.

[8]  Taylor, T. (1991) *The Life of St Samson of Dol.* Llanerch Press, Felinfach.

[9]  Warry, King, C. (1902) *Old Portland Traditions.* Dorset County Museum, Dorchester.

[10]  Haagensen, E. and Lincoln, H. (2000) *The Templars' Secret Island.* Windrush Press, Moreton-in-Marsh.

[11]  *Grimm's Law.* http://en.wikipedia.org/wiki/grimm's_law.

[12]  Waddell, L.A. (1924) *The Phoenician Origin of Britons, Scots and Anglo-Saxons.* Williams and Norgate, London. Reprinted 1990 by Banton Press, Largs.

[13]  Michell, J. (2000) *The Temple at Jerusalem: A Revelation.* Gothic Image, Glastonbury.

[14]  Pearce, White, E., White, King Warry, C.J., Edwards, J.M. and Legg, R. (1983) *Old Portland.* Dorset Publishing Company, Wincanton.

## Chapter 9

[1]  Williamson, R. (1999, 2003) *Who Were the Anglo-Saxons?* Regia Anglorum Publications, Bristol, http://www.regia.org/saxon1.htm.

[2]  Warry, King, C. (1902) *Old Portland Traditions.* Dorset County Museum, Dorchester.

[3]  Procopius. *History of the Wars.* Translated by H.B. Dewing (1914). Heinemann, Cambridge, Massachusetts. Book Jungle reproduced 2008.

[4]  Assembly of Yahweh, Cascade (undated) *The Word 'Jew' and the Scriptures.* http://assemblyoftrueisrael.com/truthpage/the_word_jew.html.

[5]  Davidiy, Y. (1993) *The Tribes: The Israelite Origins of Western Peoples*, 3rd edn. www.britam.org.

[6]  Baucum, W. (undated) *Tracing Dan.* http://www.uhcg.org/lost-10-tribes/tracing-danintro.html.

[7]  Raymond Capt, E. (1985) *Missing Links Discovered in Assyrian Tablets.* Artisan Publishers, Muskogee, Oklahoma.

[8]  Plutarch (1920) *The Parallel Lives: The Life of Marius.* Vol. IX. Loeb Classical Library, Harvard University Press, Cambridge, Massachusetts.

[9]  Turner, S. (1841) *History of the Anglo-Saxons.* Carey and Hart, Philadelphia.

[10]  Millar, A. (1991) *Treasures from Bible Times.* Chariot Victor Publishing, Colorado Springs.

## Chapter 10

1   Taylor, H. *History as Science*. Cited in Insole, A. (1952) *Immortal Britain*. The Aquarian Press, London.

2   *Somerset & Dorset, Notes & Queries*, Vol. 1, pp. 140–143. Available at Dorset Museum, Dorchester, and http://www.westcountrygenealogy.com/somerset/sdnq.htm.

3   Milton, J. (1670) *History of England*, Book IV, p. 11.

4   Numerous sources including Geoffrey of Monmouth (1984) *The History of the Kings of Britain*. The Folio Society, London.

5   Gordon, E.O. (1932). *Prehistoric London, Its Mounds and Circles*. Covenant Publishing, London.

6   Brown, T. (1970) *Trojans in the West Country*. Toucan Press, Croydon.

7   Morris, J. (1980) *'Nennius' British History and the Welsh Annals*. Phillimore, London.

8   Thorpe, L. (1966) *The History of the Kings of Britain*, translated. Introduction to Geoffrey of Monmouth, p.17. Penguin Books, London.

9   *A Trojan Connection with Britain*. Official Journal of the Ensign Trust, http://www.ensignmessage.com/archives/trojanconnection.html.

10  Roberts, P. (1811) *The Chronicle of the Kings of Britain, translated from the Welsh copy attributed to Tysilio*. Photo reduced reprint 2000. Llanerch Press, Burnham-on-Sea.

11  Bettey, J.H. (1970) *The Island and Royal Manor of Portland, 1750–1851*. J.H. Bettey, Portland.

12  Ellis, H. (1846 (ed.) *Polydore Vergil's English History: Vol. 1*. Camden Society, London.

12a Russell, P. (1964) *The Good Town of Totnes*. Devonshire Association, Exeter.

13  Morris, S. (1982) *Index of Portland Place Names*. Stuart, Morris, Portland. Available in Archive of Dorset Museum, Dorchester.

14  Waddell, L.A. (1924) *The Phoenician Origin of Britons, Scots and Anglo-Saxons*. Williams and Norgate, London. Reprinted 1990 by Banton Press, Largs.

15  Risdon, T. (1723, 1811) *Survey on the County of Devon*. Rees and Curtis, London.

16  Bowles, Lisle, W. (1828, 2007) *Hermes Britannicus: A Dissertation on the Celtic Deity, Teutates, the Mercurius of Caesar, in Further Proof and Corroboration of the Origin and Designation of the Great Temple at Abury*. Kessinger Publishing, Whitefish, Montana.

17  Pennick, N. (1998) *Celtic Sacred Landscapes*. Thames and Hudson, London.

18  Waring, E. (1977) *Ghosts and Legends of the Dorset Countryside*. Compton Press, Tisbury.

18a Castleton, R. (1996) *The Cerne Giant*. Dorset Publishing Company, Wincanton.

19  Hutchins, J. (1774) *The History and Antiquities of Dorset*. Dorchester Reference Library, Dorchester.

20  Pennie, J.F. (1827) *The Tale of a Modern Genius*. J. Andrews, London.

21  Matthews, J. and Matthews, C. (1988) *British and Irish Mythology: An Encyclopaedia of British and Irish Myth and Legend*. Aquarian Press, London.

22  Roberts, A. (1978) *Sowers of Thunder*. Rider, London.

23  Norvil, R. (1979) *Giants, the Vanished Race of Mighty Men*. Aquarian Press, London.

24  Saward, J. (2003) *Labyrinths and Mazes*. Gaia, London.

25  Eardley-Wilmot, H. (1995) *The Overland Way: From Porlock to Portland in the Bronze Age? An Investigation.* Westcountry Books, Tiverton.

26  Holinshed, R. (1587) *Chronicles of England, Scotland and Ireland*, 6 vols. Reprinted 1807 for J. Johnson and others, London. Facsimile reprint 1965 by AMS Press, New York.

## Chapter 11

1   Pennick, N. (1996) *Celtic Sacred Landscapes.* Thames & Hudson, London.

2   Maltwood, K.E. (1929) *A Guide to Glastonbury's Temple of the Stars.* James Clark, Cambridge.

3   Michell, J. (1978) Caer Sidi: The Zodiac Temples of South Britain. In: *Glastonbury: Ancient Avalon, New Jerusalem* (ed. A. Roberts), Chapter 4. Rider and Co., London.

4   Jefferies, S. (1996) *Cornwall's Landscape Giant.* Elderberry Books, St Keverne.

5   Plutarch (AD 46–127) *The Life of Demetrius.* Cited in Insole, A. (1952) *Immortal Britain*, p. 61. The Aquarian Press, London.

6   Tacitus (2003) *The Annals & The Histories (Modern Library Classics).* www.modernlibrary.com.

7   Graves, R. (1948) *The White Goddess.* Farrar, Straus and Giroux, New York.

8   Michell, J. (1969) *The New View Over Atlantis.* Thames and Hudson, London.

9   Broadhurst, P. and Miller, H. (2000) *The Dance of the Dragon.* Pendragon Press, Hillsdale, New York.

10  Biltcliffe, G. (2008) *The Belinus Line UK.* www.belinusline.com.

11  Reader's Digest (1973) *Folklore, Myths and Legends of Britain.* Reader's Digest, London.

12  McNeill, F.M. (1990) *An Iona Anthology.* New Iona Press, Strathpeffer.

13  Michell, J. (1994) *At the Centre of the World: Polar Symbolism Discovered in Celtic, Norse and Other Ritualized Landscapes.* Thames and Hudson, London.

14  Parker Pearson, M. (2000) Great sites: Llyn Cerrig Bach. *British Archaeology*, 53. http://www.britarch.ac.uk/ba/ba53/ba53feat.html.

15  Jones, G. and Jones, J. (translators) (1949) *The Mabinogion (Everyman Classics).* J.M. Dent and Sons, London.

## Appendix A

1   Morris, S. (1985) *Portland, an Illustrated History.* Dovecote Press, Wimborne.

2   *Veasta: The Sea Monster of Chesil Beach.* http://www.users.globalnet.co.uk/~wykedh/veasta.htm.

3   Dark Dorset (2009) http://www.darkdorset.co.uk/.

4   Waring, E. (1977) *Ghosts and Legends of the Dorset Countryside.* Compton Press, Tisbury.

5   Hymas, M. (1981) *Dorset Folklore.* Books of Wessex, Taunton.

6   Palmer, S. (1998) *Ancient Portland – Archaeology of the Isle.* Susann Palmer, Portland.

## Appendix B

1   Holinshed, R. (1587) *Chronicles of England, Scotland and Ireland*, 6 vols. Reprinted 1807 for J. Johnson and others, London. Facsimile reprint 1965 by AMS Press, New York.

# *The Spine of Albion*

## Coming soon, the second book by Gary Biltcliffe

The culmination of 15 years' research of Britain's longest alignment
of ancient sites – the Belinus Line.

Beginning at the Isle of Wight, Britain's Magical Island, this cosmic axis travels through ancient centres of kingship: Winchester, the old capital

Belinus Line

of England; Carlisle, capital of the north; Dunfermline, ancient capital of Scotland; as well as many important prehistoric sites and Celtic centres of power, ending at Durness on the north coast of Scotland.

The Belinus Line is the north–south equivalent of the famous St Michael Line which stretches from Land's End in Cornwall to Hopton-on-Sea on the Norfolk coast. It also exhibits the same earth energy currents first discovered by dowser Hamish Millar that weave around the alignment, one female (yin) and the other masculine (yang). The ancient Chinese called these lines *lung mei* – the Dragon's breath – pathways of connective consciousness between the land and her people.

Gary's research of this line and its associated energies reveals a sacred middle route through Britain highlighted by mysterious hillforts built during the Iron Age when the alignment targeted the setting of the giant star Deneb in the constellation of Cygnus, the swan. Many ancient cultures around the world revered this star as the portal to the realm of the gods or the afterlife. Was the Belinus Line the sacred pathway to the gods?

The in-depth investigative work carried out by Gary and his partner Caroline Hoare includes such topics as archaeology, hidden history and folklore, giving new insights for the reader into the very 'matter of Britain' and its inhabitants. It will certainly please those who wish to explore the more sacred aspects of the British landscape and its great heritage.

# Portland Museum

**PORTLAND MUSEUM™**

The Portland Museum is based in two thatched 17th century cottages in Wakeham, above Church Ope Cove, one of which was a location used by Thomas Hardy in his novel *The Wellbeloved*. The Museum had a major makeover for 2009 with new displays based on Stone, Sea, Local Archaeology and Famous People. There are exhibitions on shipwrecks, the history of stone, fossil collections, local archaeology, and Dr Marie Stopes, the famous birth control pioneer who gifted the cottages to the people of Portland in 1930. You can also enjoy the garden, picnic area, refreshments and shop. The Museum houses a number of artefacts discussed in *The Spirit of Portland*, such as sarcophagi, the stone head, Reeve staffs and many stone remains from St Andrew's Church. It is a 'must visit' for anyone wishing to follow-up on Gary's research.

*For more info tel: 01305 821804 or email: portlandmuseum@googlemail.com.*

# Portland Sculpture and Quarry Trust

Portland is one of the most intensively quarried areas in the UK – there were once over one hundred working quarries on the island, now there are just six. Facing the social issues connected with disused and neglected quarries, local residents formed the Portland Sculpture and Quarry Trust in 1983 and, through artists giving work back to the quarries, created a new model for quarry regeneration in Tout Quarry. This model is now being applied to the regeneration of the Drill Hall and Independent Quarry, bringing together geology, ecology and culture, and shows how a community working in partnership with artists, designers, education and industry can jointly shape the design and sustainable after-use of the quarry landscape. The site will be a resource for sharing knowledge, skills and creativity, where the past informs the future, a place to learn, and enable people to interact with 150 million years of earth history and radiate new energy and interest.

*If you would like to know more about the Trust or Tout Quarry Stone Carving /Sculpture Workshops, visit www.learningstone.org or contact The Drill Hall, Easton Lane, tel: 01305 826736, email: psqt@learningstone.org.*

# Filming on Portland

Claire and Duncan of The Light and Energy Channel spent a fabulous day with Gary filming at some of the many wonderful and interesting sites discussed in *The Spirit of Portland*.

  *'Gary has discovered such a wealth of information about the Isle of Portland that is so important to share, not only in this time but for the generations to come. This sacred isle with all its secret history both archaeological and spiritual should be protected and respected. We at The Light and Energy Channel were so pleased to work with Gary and be a small part of helping him impart his knowledge to those around the world.'*

To see the film visit

http://www.thelightandenergychannel.tv/the-spirit-of-portland-with-gary-biltcliffe/

The Light and Energy Channel is a web-based TV show creating an online community that can enjoy regular video shows covering all aspects of Mind, Body and Spirit, created by Claire Whiles, lecturer, nutritional therapist and healer, and Duncan Smith New Media. Subjects covered in the shows include nutrition, conspiracies, ancient sites, crystals, astrology, crop circles, dowsing, new science, paranormal activity and much more. The shows take a variety of formats, from demonstrations, interviews and discussions to filming on location at sacred sites. The shows are watched throughout the world and can be accessed via www.thelightandenergychannel.tv or ITunes completely free of charge. The shows are also aired on Sky 200 Edge Media.

# Lesser Known Weymouth

### by Julie Musk

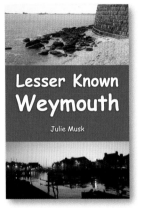

This book looks at the quirkier side of Weymouth – rather like having your own local guide to show you around and point out the interesting bits. It's essentially a contemporary look, highlighting local people, businesses and organisations that are unique or special to the area. Stories and anecdotes are usually more interesting than facts, and this book hopes above all to be a good story. Interviews with local people are interspersed with background details and personal observations. It includes walks, with quiz questions to keep younger readers interested. Like its companion *Lesser Known Swanage*, in describing what's going on behind the scenes, it is an essential practical guide for anyone who wants to fully appreciate this 'Olympic' seaside town.

*Full colour, 160 pages including 120 photos, 8 detailed maps and 6 exploratory walks round town. Priced £10.99 from Roving Press*

# Secret Places of West Dorset

### by Louise Hodgson

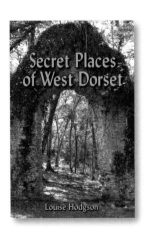

The book describes over 40 less-frequented places to visit in West Dorset, ranging from a holy well at Morcombelake, haunted Coney's Castle and screaming skull at Bettiscombe, stone circles at Abbotsbury, plague burials and posy tree at Mapperton, and our hidden ancestors at Long Bredy. Exploring Dorset's folklore, curiosities, legends and history, tucked away churches, ancient trackways, liminal places and megaliths, author Louise Hodgson takes you on a personal tour, revealing the beauty, magic and importance of the landscape. The book is illustrated with 94 colour photographs and 10 of Louise's own watercolour paintings.

*Full colour, 144 pages including 94 photos, 10 watercolour paintings by the author and 1 area map. Priced £12.95 from Roving Press*

# Other Roving Press Titles

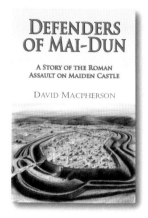

DEFENDERS OF MAI-DUN

A STORY OF THE ROMAN ASSAULT ON MAIDEN CASTLE

DAVID MACPHERSON

Roaring Dorset!
Encounters with Big Cats

Merrily Harpur

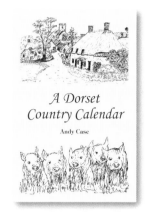

A Dorset Country Calendar

Andy Case

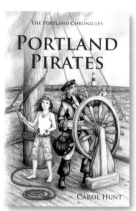

THE PORTLAND CHRONICLES

PORTLAND PIRATES

CAROL HUNT

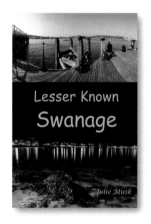

Lesser Known Swanage

Julie Musk

THE PORTLAND CHRONICLES

THE PORTLAND SEA DRAGON

CAROL HUNT

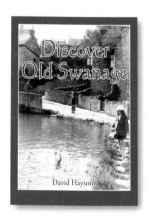

Discover Old Swanage

David Haysom

Kids' Dorset

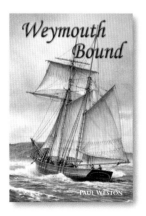

Weymouth Bound

PAUL WESTON

Roving Press

*If you like exploring, you'll love our books*

# Index